JUNiOR DRUG AWARENESS

Inhalants and Solvents

JUNIOR DRUG AWARENESS

Alcohol

Amphetamines and
Other Stimulants

Cocaine and Crack

Diet Pills

Marijuana

Ecstasy and Other Club Drugs

Nicotine

Heroin

Over-the-Counter Drugs

How to Say No to Drugs

Prozac and Other
Antidepressants

Inhalants and Solvents

Steroids and Other
Performance-Enhancing
Drugs

Vicodin, OxyContin, and
Other Pain Relievers

JUNIOR DRUG AWARENESS

Inhalants and Solvents

Tara Koellhoffer

CHELSEA HOUSE
PUBLISHERS

An imprint of Infobase Publishing

Junior Drug Awareness: Inhalants and Solvents
Copyright © 2008 by Infobase Publishing

Chelsea House
An imprint of Infobase Publishing
132 West 31st Street
New York NY 10001

Library of Congress Cataloging-in-Publication Data

Koellhoffer, Tara.
  Inhalants and solvents / Tara Koellhoffer.
    p. cm. — (Junior drug awareness)
  Includes bibliographical references and index.
  ISBN 978-0-7910-9698-7 (hardcover)
  1. Solvent abuse—Juvenile literature. I. Title. II. Series.

  RC568.S64K63 2008
  362.29'9—dc22   2007024824

Chelsea House books are available at special discounts when purchased in
bulk quantities for businesses, associations, institutions, or sales promotions.
Please call our Special Sales Department in New York at (212) 967-8800 or
(800) 322-8755.

You can find Chelsea House on the World Wide Web
at http://www.chelseahouse.com

Text design by Erik Lindstrom
Cover design by Jooyoung An

Printed in the United States of America

Bang NMSG 10 9 8 7 6 5 4 3 2 1

This book is printed on acid-free paper.

All links and web addresses were checked and verified to be correct at the time of
publication. Because of the dynamic nature of the web, some addresses and links
may have changed since publication and may no longer be valid.

CONTENTS

INTRODUCTION
Battling a Pandemic: A History of Drugs
in the United States   6
by Ronald J. Brogan,
Regional Director of D.A.R.E. America

1   Introduction to Inhalants and Solvents   12

2   The History of Inhalant Use   24

3   What Are Inhalants and Solvents?   34

4   Inhalants' Effects on the Body   45

5   Why People Use Inhalants   58

6   Abuse and Addiction   67

7   Getting Help and Preventing
    Inhalant Abuse   73

    Glossary   94

    Bibliography   99

    Further Reading   105

    Picture Credits   106

    Index   107

    About the Authors   112

Battling a Pandemic: A History of Drugs in the United States

When Johnny came marching home again after the Civil War, he probably wasn't marching in a very straight line. This is because Johnny, like 400,000 of his fellow drug-addled soldiers, was addicted to morphine. With the advent of morphine and the invention of the hypodermic needle, drug addiction became a prominent problem during the nineteenth century. It was the first time such widespread drug dependence was documented in history.

Things didn't get much better in the later decades of the nineteenth century. Cocaine and opiates were used as over-the-counter "medicines." Of course, the most famous was Coca-Cola, which actually did contain cocaine in its early days.

After the turn of the twentieth century, drug abuse was spiraling out of control, and the United States government stepped in with the first regulatory controls. In 1906, the Pure Food and Drug Act became a law. It required the labeling of product ingredients. Next came the Harrison Narcotics Tax Act of 1914, which outlawed illegal importation or distribution of cocaine and opiates. During this time, neither the medical community nor the general population was aware of the principles of addiction.

After the passage of the Harrison Act, drug addiction was not a major issue in the United States until the 1960s, when drug abuse became a much bigger social problem. During this time, the federal government's drug enforcement agencies were found to be ineffective. Organizations often worked against one another, causing counterproductive effects. By 1973, things had gotten so bad that President Richard Nixon, by executive order, created the Drug Enforcement Administration (DEA), which became the lead agency in all federal narcotics investigations. It continues in that role to this day. The effectiveness of enforcement and the so-called "Drug War" are open to debate. Cocaine use has been reduced by 75% since its peak in 1985. However, its replacement might be methamphetamine (speed, crank, crystal), which is arguably more dangerous and is now plaguing the country. Also, illicit drugs tend to be cyclical, with various drugs, such as LSD, appearing, disappearing, and then reappearing again. It is probably closest to the truth to say that a war on drugs can never be won, just managed.

Fighting drugs involves a three-pronged battle. Enforcement is one prong. Education and prevention is the second. Treatment is the third.

Although pandemics of drug abuse have been with us for more than 150 years, education and prevention were not seriously considered until the 1970s. In 1982, former First Lady Betty Ford made drug treatment socially acceptable with the opening of the Betty Ford Center. This followed her own battle with addiction. Other treatment centers—including Hazelton, Fair Oaks, and Smithers (now called the Addiction Institute of New York)—added to the growing number of clinics, and soon detox facilities were in almost every city. The cost of a single day in one of these facilities is often more than $1,000, and the effectiveness of treatment centers is often debated. To this day, there is little regulation over who can practice counseling.

It soon became apparent that the most effective way to deal with the drug problem was prevention by education. By some estimates, the overall cost of drug abuse to society exceeds $250 billion per year; preventive education is certainly the most cost-effective way to deal with the problem. Drug education can save people from misery, pain, and ultimately even jail time or death. In the early 1980s, First Lady Nancy Reagan started the "Just Say No" program. Although many scoffed at the program, its promotion of total abstinence from drugs has been effective with many adolescents. In the late 1980s, drug education was not science based, and people essentially were throwing mud at the wall to see what would stick. Motivations of all types spawned hundreds, if not thousands, of drug-education programs. Promoters of some programs used whatever political clout they could muster to get on various government agencies' lists of most effective programs. The bottom line, however, is that prevention is very difficult to quantify. It's nearly impossible to prove that drug use would have occurred if it were not prevented from happening.

In 1983, the Los Angeles Unified School District, in conjunction with the Los Angeles Police Department, started what was considered at that time to be the gold standard of school-based drug education programs. The program was called Drug Abuse Resistance Education, otherwise known as D.A.R.E. The program called for specially trained police officers to deliver drug-education programs in schools. This was an era in which community-oriented policing was all the rage. The logic was that kids would give street credibility to a police officer who spoke to them about drugs. The popularity of the program was unprecedented. It spread all across the country and around the world. Ultimately, 80% of American school districts would utilize the program. Parents, police officers, and kids all loved it. Unexpectedly, a special bond was formed between the kids who took the program and the police officers who ran it. Even in adulthood, many kids remember the name of their D.A.R.E. officer.

By 1991, national drug use had been halved. In any other medical-oriented field, this figure would be astonishing. The number of people in the United States using drugs went from about 25 million in the early 1980s to 11 million in 1991. All three prongs of the battle against drugs vied for government dollars, with each prong claiming credit for the reduction in drug use. There is no doubt that each contributed to the decline in drug use, but most people agreed that preventing drug abuse before it started had proved to be the most effective strategy. The National Institute on Drug Abuse (NIDA), which was established in 1974, defines its mandate in this way: "NIDA's mission is to lead the Nation in bringing the power of science to bear on drug abuse and addiction." NIDA leaders were the experts in prevention and treatment, and they had enormous resources. In

1986, the nonprofit Partnership for a Drug-Free America was founded. The organization defined its mission as, "Putting to use all major media outlets, including TV, radio, print advertisements and the Internet, along with the pro bono work of the country's best advertising agencies." The Partnership for a Drug-Free America is responsible for the popular campaign that compared "your brain on drugs" to fried eggs.

The American drug problem was front-page news for years up until 1990–1991. Then the Gulf War took over the news, and drugs never again regained the headlines. Most likely, this lack of media coverage has led to some peaks and valleys in the number of people using drugs, but there has not been a return to anything near the high percentage of use recorded in 1985. According to the University of Michigan's 2006 Monitoring the Future study, which measured adolescent drug use, there were 840,000 fewer American kids using drugs in 2006 than in 2001. This represents a 23% reduction in drug use. With the exception of prescription drugs, drug use continues to decline.

In 2000, the Robert Wood Johnson Foundation recognized that the D.A.R.E. Program, with its tens of thousands of trained police officers, had the top state-of-the-art delivery system of drug education in the world. The foundation dedicated $15 million to develop a cutting-edge prevention curriculum to be delivered by D.A.R.E. The new D.A.R.E. program incorporates the latest in prevention and education, including high-tech, interactive, and decision-model-based approaches. D.A.R.E. officers are trained as "coaches" who support kids as they practice research-based refusal strategies in high-stakes peer-pressure environments. Through stunning magnetic resonance imaging (MRI) images, students get to see tangible proof of how various substances diminish brain activity.

Will this program be the solution to the drug problem in the United States? By itself, probably not. It is simply an integral part of a larger equation that everyone involved hopes will prevent kids from ever starting to use drugs. The equation also requires guidance in the home, without which no program can be effective.

Ronald J. Brogan
Regional Director
D.A.R.E America

1

Introduction to Inhalants and Solvents

One afternoon in the summer of 2004, 14-year-old Katelyne Fries was hanging out with some friends in her hometown of Fort Drum, New York. One of her friends brought out a can of dust cleaner and said he was going to show everybody something cool. He put the can's nozzle in his mouth and inhaled. Then he started talking in a low voice that sounded to Katelyne like Darth Vader. All the teens thought it was hilarious, so they all tried inhaling from the aerosol can, too. Thinking it was just harmless fun, Katelyne and her friends tried **huffing** again several times over the next year. But the next summer, Katelyne learned something that changed her mind about inhaling household products. She read a news story on the Internet about Kyle

Household cleaning products contain just some of the chemicals people abuse as inhalants and solvents.

Williams, the 14-year-old son of a police officer who died from **sudden sniffing death syndrome** after inhaling a chemical product. Kyle was found dead. The straw that he'd been using to sniff was still hanging from his mouth. Like Katelyne, Kyle thought that huffing was safe, that he was only inhaling compressed air. Kyle never realized that he was inhaling chemicals that could—and did—kill him.

WHAT ARE INHALANTS?

Inhalants include any fume, vapor, or gas that is inhaled in order to get high. Inhalant abuse often is not

PROFILE OF THE AVERAGE INHALANT USER

Inhalant users come from all segments of society, from different social classes and different age groups. However, children and teens are the most common users, with peak usage occurring around eighth grade.

According to the 2005 Youth Risk Behavior Surveillance System Survey, 13.4% of Caucasian youth claimed to be inhalant users. Among Hispanic Americans, 13.0% were inhalant users, and 6.8% of African American youth said they used inhalants. Although more young people have tried smoking (54.3%), drinking alcohol (74.3%), and marijuana (38.4%), inhalant use is a growing problem.

The Substance Abuse and Mental Health Service Administration's (SAMHSA) 2004 National Survey on Drug Use and Health indicates that 75% of first-time inhalant users are under the age of 18. Among young people in grades 4 through 6 and 10 through 12, boys use inhalants at slightly higher rates than girls, but boys and girls in grades 7 through 9 abuse inhalant drugs at about the same rate. Users over the age of 18 are almost always male.

Inhalants often are the first drug a young person tries. Many young people try inhalants even before they try drinking alcohol. Inhalant abuse is much more common than most people realize. More than 12% of high school students have tried inhalants at least once. About 8.5% have tried hallucinogenic drugs, and about 6.3% have tried Ecstasy.

People almost always use inhalants while in groups—at least at first. Once a user has become accustomed to using inhalants or becomes addicted, he or she often will begin to use the substances alone.

considered as serious as the abuse of other drugs, such as cocaine and marijuana. Yet, inhalants are very dangerous and widely used. About one out of every four school-age children in the United States admit to trying some type of inhalant. In the United Kingdom, there have been reports that at least one person dies each week from abusing inhalants.

It is not surprising that inhalants are so frequently used. About 1,400 products can be abused this way. And almost all of them are found in typical households. The average home usually has 30 bathroom and kitchen products that can be abused as inhalants.

Because they all have legal uses, inhalants are inexpensive and easy to get. That means that the people who use them often are much younger than people who abuse other drugs. The average age of an inhalant user is around 12 or 13. But there have been reports of children as young as 6 trying inhalants.

THE MOST COMMON INHALANTS

Inhalants include any kind of chemical or **solvent** that can be used to get high. When they are abused, inhalants are considered drugs. Inhalants affect the brain and can change a person's perceptions of the world. Inhalants can be **sedative**, **hypnotic**, and/or **anesthetic** drugs. Many inhalants have multiple effects. When inhaled, the chemical fumes go straight to the heart, lungs, and bloodstream, affecting the **nervous system** and especially the brain. Because they hit the brain rapidly, without first going through the **digestive system**, kidneys, or liver, inhalants can be more powerful than many other drugs.

Inhalants also are considered **poisons**. They are household products that are not intended to be consumed. In fact, they can kill if ingested.

It's easy to ignore warning labels, but they often provide essential information about the dangers of inhaling or swallowing common products.

There are several types of inhalants, including **volatile solvents**, **aerosols**, gases, and **nitrites**. If you see any of the following ingredients listed on the label of a household product, it is something that potentially can be abused as an inhalant.

- *Acetone:* Often found in rubber cement, permanent markers, and nail polish remover
- *Butane:* Often found in gasoline, hairspray, spray paint, deodorant, air freshening sprays, and lighter fluid
- *Chlorinated hydrocarbons:* Often found in correction fluid, stain removers, and dry-cleaning chemicals
- *Fluorocarbons:* Often found in hairspray, air fresheners, spray paint, and pain-killing sprays
- *Propane:* Often found in air freshening sprays, deodorant, and spray paint
- *Toluene:* Often found in airplane glue, paint thinner, and spray paint

Volatile Solvents

Volatile solvents include household or industrial solvents, art and office supply solvents, and other solvent-containing products. Most of these products are **organic** solvents. That is, they are liquid **carbon** compounds that can react with other **compounds**. They also evaporate easily into gases or can be sprayed in aerosols. Organic solvents are some of the easiest inhalants to buy, and they can be some of the most dangerous ones to abuse. Some of the most common organic solvents are paint thinners, paint removers, glue, the fluid in felt-tip markers, correction fluid, lighter fluid, hairspray, nail polish remover, and gasoline.

Nitrites

Nitrites are nitrogen compounds. When inhaled, they act as **vasodilators**: They relax the walls of blood vessels, causing the vessels to widen. These compounds are used in medicine. They can increase blood flow by making blood vessels wider. This can help ease chest pain caused by a lack of blood flow to the heart. When used as recreational drugs, nitrites depress the **central nervous system**. This makes the user feel giddy and lightheaded. The most common nitrites are amyl nitrite and butyl nitrite. Both are yellowish liquids. When prescribed for chest pain, amyl nitrite usually comes in glass or plastic capsules called "poppers" that can be crushed. The liquid evaporates and the gas is inhaled. Butyl nitrite normally comes in a spray can or bottle that is sold as an air freshener.

Gases

Many gases can be abused as inhalants. They include household and commercial products, such as propane tanks, butane lighters, whipped cream dispensers, and gases that are used to keep refrigerators cool. Other commonly abused gases include medical anesthetics, such as nitrous oxide, chloroform, ether, and halothane. Nitrous oxide, often called "laughing gas," has been used as a recreational inhalant since the mid-1800s. Today, it is used frequently as a sedative for dental procedures. It also is the gas used in canned whipped cream.

HOW ARE INHALANTS USED?

Inhalants can be ingested in several ways. They can be sniffed or snorted from the container in which they are packaged, or the vapors can be sprayed into the nose

Inhalant huffing and sniffing by homeless children on the streets of Bucharest, Romania, is a major problem that government officials hope to stop. These children spend most of their time sniffing glue, stealing, and running from police. The glassy-eyed boy in this image, from December 2006, has just sniffed glue.

or mouth. This is how most organic solvents are used. Other inhalants, particularly liquid solvents, can be "huffed." The user holds a chemical-soaked rag up to his or her face and breathes in. Inhalants also can be "bagged": sprayed onto a piece of plastic that the user sniffs, or sprayed into a paper bag that the user places over his or her nose and mouth. Some users spray chemicals onto sleeves or other parts of their clothing so they can breathe in the vapors throughout the day. Others spray chemicals into soda cans and then inhale the vapors. In some cases, balloons are filled with nitrous oxide or helium, which is then inhaled directly. Amyl nitrite capsules are crushed and held up to the nose, while butyl nitrite may be applied to cloth or paper or inhaled from its container.

There are a few other, somewhat stranger, methods of abusing inhalants. The user may apply the product to fingernails and then put the fingers in the mouth or nose to breathe the fumes. This is usually done with correction fluids. Some users douse a bandanna or scarf in the chemical and then tie it over the nose and mouth. Others actually put the inhalant-soaked cloth in their mouths. Some inhalant abusers soak cotton swabs with chemicals and then stuff them in their nostrils.

DANGERS OF INADVERTENT USE

Although inhalants are some of the most widely abused drugs in the United States, they are not listed on the schedules of illegal drugs categorized by the Controlled Substances Act of 1970. That's because they are included in household cleaners and other products. However, inhalants can be extremely dangerous, and not only to people who deliberately abuse them. The fumes given off by chemical products can cause an accidental high. In rare cases, people using these products for their intended uses will inhale too many of the vapors and become ill or even die. Read the warning labels on any product that contains inhalants. See a doctor or go to the hospital if your eyes or throat become irritated, if you begin coughing, or if you develop a headache or feel sick to your stomach.

THE CONTROLLED SUBSTANCES ACT

The Controlled Substances Act of 1970 places all drugs into one of five categories, or schedules, depending on their uses and their potential for abuse.

SCHEDULE I:
- The drug or other substance has a high potential for abuse.
- The drug or other substance has no currently accepted medical use in the United States.
- The drug or other substance is not safe for use, even under medical supervision.
- Examples of Schedule I drugs include Ecstasy, GHB, heroin, and LSD.

SCHEDULE II:
- The drug or other substance has a high potential for abuse.
- The drug or other substance has a currently accepted medical use in the United States, but there may be severe restrictions.
- Abuse of the drug or other substance may easily lead to **addiction**.
- Examples of Schedule II drugs include morphine, Ritalin, phencyclidine (PCP), and methadone.

(continues on page 22)

(continued from page 21)

SCHEDULE III:

- The drug or other substance has a potential for abuse, but it's lower than the potential of drugs or other substances in Schedules I and II.
- The drug or other substance has a currently accepted medical use in the United States.
- Abuse of the drug or other substance may lead to moderate or low physical dependence or high psychological dependence.
- Examples of Schedule III drugs include anabolic steroids, codeine, and some barbiturates.

SCHEDULE IV:

- The drug or other substance has a lower potential for abuse than drugs or other substances in Schedule III.
- The drug or other substance has a currently accepted medical use in the United States.
- Abuse of the drug or other substance may lead to addiction, but the addiction is not as severe as that seen with the drugs or substances in Schedule III.
- Examples of Schedule IV drugs include phenobarbital, Xanax, and Valium.

SCHEDULE V:

- The drug or other substance has a lower potential for abuse than the drugs or other substances in Schedule IV.

- The drug or other substance has a currently accepted medical use in the United States.
- Abuse of the drug or other substance may lead to addiction, but the addiction is not as severe as that seen with the drugs or substances in Schedule IV.
- Examples of Schedule V drugs include cough suppressants.

2

The History of Inhalant Use

Although inhalants have become more popular than ever over the past several years, they are not new. People have been using inhalants to get high since ancient times.

INHALANTS IN ANCIENT TIMES
In ancient Greece, the priestess Themis presided over the oracle of Apollo at Delphi. This woman was believed to speak on behalf of the gods, and people traveled from all over Greece and other parts of the world to ask her questions. Usually, her answers were confusing and rambling. She seemed to be speaking while in a trance. Those who believed in her powers thought the gods were speaking through her and were giving hints

The Grecian figure Aegeus consults the oracle of Delphi with the help of the priestess Themis, around 440 BC.

about the future in the form of riddles or metaphors. A few people, however, believed that the oracle was not speaking for the gods. Instead, they thought she was **intoxicated** on fumes that were rising up from a chamber below the floor.

For centuries, scientists searched for the source of the oracle's visions. Finally, in the 1990s, a team of scientists discovered geological **faults** in the rocks under the oracle's temple. Through the cracks in these rocks, a sweet-smelling gas called ethylene most likely drifted up. This caused the oracle to experience **euphoria** and **hallucinations**.

Inhalants—including gases and the smoke from incense and other burned substances—have long been used in many cultures as part of religious rituals. Native American **shamans** were known to inhale substances that caused hallucinations. In ancient Egypt and the Middle East, altars have been found with special places carved out to hold burning incense that had **psychoactive** effects.

INHALED ANESTHETICS

In the late thirteenth century, **ether** was discovered by a Spanish chemist named Raymundus Lullius. Called "sweet vitriol" at the time, ether was used for its hypnotic effects and to relieve pain. Doctors also used ether to treat illnesses, including **scurvy** and problems with the lungs. By the mid-nineteenth century, doctors began to use ether to prevent patients from feeling the pain of surgery. The first known surgical use of ether occurred in March 1842 (although a study of the work wasn't published until 1849), when Dr. Crawford Long of Georgia removed two tumors from the neck of his patient, James Venable. Dr. Long used ether and Mr. Venable slept through the procedure.

Like most drugs, ether could be abused—and people found ways to do so. Throughout the nineteenth century, there were reports of people inhaling ether in large quantities—as much as a pint per day—because they liked how it made them feel: relaxed and happy. Some people even used ether to help them sleep.

American Crawford Long was a surgeon and a pioneer in the use of ether as an anesthetic. On March 30, 1842, he gave ether to a boy before removing lumps from his neck. Although Long was the first to use ether in this way, he didn't publish the results of his work until 1849. Thus, Dr. William Morton is sometimes credited with the first use of ether in surgery.

Being able to sleep through painful operations was an important breakthrough, but ether wasn't perfect. It could irritate the lungs and throat, and many people found its odor unpleasant. Another inhaled anesthetic, called **chloroform**, was discovered in 1831. Its sleep-inducing properties were noticed in 1847. Chloroform also could irritate the lungs and throat, but its sweet smell was considered an improvement over the smell of ether. By 1871, a report in the *New York Medical Journal* said that chloroform was being used for half of the surgeries that required anesthesia.

In smaller doses than those used for surgery, chloroform produced a high that many people found enjoyable. Throughout the nineteenth century, chloroform was widely abused, often by the doctors and other scientists who used it as part of their work.

Another common inhaled anesthetic is **nitrous oxide**—often called "laughing gas." Discovered by English chemist Joseph Priestley in 1772, nitrous oxide was actually the first anesthetic ever used. However, it never became as popular as ether and chloroform, which were more powerful and easier to work with. From the time that English chemist Humphry Davy began to study nitrous oxide in 1800, the gas was much more popular as a recreational drug than as an anesthetic. In fact, many doctors and scientists—including Davy—threw parties and demonstrations at which guests enjoyed the effects of inhaled nitrous oxide.

At one of these demonstrations, an American dentist named Horace Wells witnessed a man injuring himself while high on nitrous oxide. The man reported feeling no pain when he got a severe gash on his leg. Wells realized that if nitrous oxide could prevent the man from feeling his wound, it also might dull the pain of pulling teeth. Wells set up a demonstration in which he pulled a tooth after giving his patient nitrous oxide. Unfortunately, Wells did not give the patient enough gas, and the patient screamed out in pain. The disappointed audience booed Wells and dismissed his notion of using nitrous oxide as an anesthetic in dentistry. Wells

NITROUS OXIDE PARTIES

After nitrous oxide was discovered in the late 1700s, many people saw inhaling it as a cheap and safe alternative to drinking alcohol. Some of the main advocates of nitrous oxide were scientists—including Humphry Davy, the first to study the gas. Davy often held parties where all the guests inhaled large amounts of nitrous oxide to get high. Some celebrities of the day, such as poet Samuel Taylor Coleridge and Peter Roget (who developed *Roget's Thesaurus*), attended these parties.

The nitrous oxide parties were such a success that Davy and other scientists considered marketing the gas as a recreational drug. They believed that they could supply it to consumers in bags and charge less than the price of alcoholic beverages. Some enterprising salesmen staged demonstrations of the drug, at which volunteers inhaled the gas and the audience witnessed them laughing, dancing, and singing.

Nitrous oxide never did replace alcohol, mainly because it wasn't as readily available and because accidents sometimes occurred when people were high on the gas. It did remain in use, however, mainly in dental offices to relieve patients' anxiety.

This caricature of an early nineteenth century chemistry lecture at the Royal Institution in London shows key figures in the early use of inhalants. At the center is Dr. Thomas Garnet (lecturer in chemistry), who is experimenting with nitrous oxide. Garnet is assisted by a young Humphry Davy (center right). The caricature's artist is James Gillray (1757–1815), an English artist who drew images to poke fun at royalty, politicians, and social situations in his day.

eventually became addicted to chloroform. In 1848, he killed himself by slitting an artery in his leg after taking a large dose of chloroform.

After Wells's death, other scientists found ways to put nitrous oxide to work. In 1933, a British doctor named Ralph Minnitt developed a machine that mixed nitrous oxide with air and delivered it to patients. The dose was large enough to relieve pain, but not so large that the patient lost consciousness. Later machines mixed nitrous oxide with oxygen, which improved the pain-relieving effects. These machines were used by pregnant women to relieve labor pain. Nitrous oxide is still used as a pain reliever for laboring women in Europe, but it's rare in the United States.

Today, the main use of nitrous oxide in this country is in dental offices. Dentists use it to make people feel less nervous. Nitrous oxide also is found in some gasoline additives and in cans of whipped cream, and many people use these everyday products to get high.

INHALANTS AS RECREATIONAL DRUGS

People continued to use nitrous oxide and other inhalants as recreational drugs throughout the nineteenth century and into the twentieth century. By the 1940s, other inhaled substances also were being used. One of the most popular was gasoline, which was more frequently abused as an inhalant as automobiles became more common. Sniffing gasoline became a compulsion for many who tried it. This provided more evidence that inhalants could be addictive.

In the 1940s and 1950s, reports of children sniffing the glue used for making model airplanes alerted the public to the problem of inhalant abuse. Toluene, the mind-altering chemical in these glues, eventually was removed from many glues and other household products in the United States. In other countries, some glues still contain toluene. Toluene also is found in other products in the United States, including gasoline and paint remover.

In the 1960s, as hippies looked for ways to alter their consciousness, drug use of all kinds—including inhalant abuse—became more widespread. Sniffing commercial products, such as paint thinner, glue, and shoe polish, became a popular and inexpensive way to get high. Over time, people discovered more substances that could be inhaled to get high. Almost all were common household products, such as aerosol cans and felt-tip markers. Because these products had legitimate uses, they were easy to get. It also was difficult for the government to regulate them or make them illegal.

INHALANT USE TODAY

In the nineteenth and early twentieth centuries, most inhalant users were adults. Many even worked in the medical field. Today, users are most often people in their early teens. Inhalants are cheaper and easier to obtain than most illicit drugs. Therefore, it's easy for young adults to abuse them.

Among teens in the United States today, inhalants are believed to be the second most popular drug. Marijuana is the first. According to the National Institute on Drug Abuse, about 23 million Americans ages 12 and older have abused an inhalant at least once. One out of every five teenagers in the United States has used inhalants to get high, and more than 2.6 million young people have experimented with some type of inhalant. Even though club drugs like Ecstasy are often seen as more immediate threats, inhalants have been tried at least once by more teens than Ecstasy and OxyContin combined.

Even more disturbing than the high rates of inhalant abuse among young people is the fact that few parents realize the dangers. As many as 44% of sixth-graders have reported abusing inhalants. However, according to an Alliance for Consumer Education study, 95% of parents don't believe their kids have used inhalants, and 47% say they have never discussed the risks of inhalant use with their preteens.

These statistics are alarming not just because so many young people are experimenting with drugs, but because inhalants can be deadly—even the first time they are used.

AN ACCIDENTAL DEATH

It may be easy for young people to use inhalants, but it's never safe. Twelve-year-old Rayshell Griffin of Pittsburgh, Pennsylvania, died in 2003 after trying to get high by huffing fumes from an aerosol air freshener.

Griffin brought the aerosol can to a party at her after-school program. An adult at the party noticed Griffin resting her head on a table with her coat covering her and asked if she was okay. She said she was all right and put her head back down. Griffin then had a seizure and died two hours later at a nearby hospital. Her clothes were soaked with air freshener and a half-empty aerosol can was found in her coat. The effects of huffing were made worse by the young girl's asthma.

A can of air freshener found with the body of Rayshell Griffin sits on a table in front of Allegheny County (Pennsylvania) coroner Dr. Cyril Wecht on December 4, 2003. Dr. Wecht spoke of the harmful effects of inhalants on the young girl's body.

3

What Are Inhalants and Solvents?

Solvents are liquids that turn to vapor at room temperature. They make up one category of inhalants. An inhalant is any substance—gas, solvent, aerosol, or nitrite—that can be inhaled to get high. There are more than 1,400 different products that can cause a high—and be physically dangerous—when inhaled. A complete list of common products that can be used as inhalant drugs can be found online at the Alliance for Consumer Education's Web site (http://www.inhalant.org).

THE MOST COMMON INHALANTS AND THEIR USES

All inhalants work directly on the central nervous system, changing the user's mood and altering the mind's perception of the world. Because they have everyday, legitimate uses, inhalants are easy to get, easy to hide, and easy to underestimate. Because inhalants are so common, many users don't realize that they are dangerous.

Gases

Several gases are among the most popular inhalants. They include nitrous oxide, butane, propane, helium, ether, chloroform, and halothane.

PRODUCTS THAT CAN BE ABUSED

- *Art Supplies:* Rubber cement, printing inks, clear finishes, spray paints
- *Auto Supplies:* Spray lubricants, degreasers, Freon, gasoline, lacquers, flat-tire-fixing products
- *Cleaning Supplies:* Aerosol air freshener sprays, computer air dusters, virtually any product packaged in an aerosol can
- *Cooking Supplies:* Whipped cream cans, cooking oil sprays
- *General Supplies:* Glues, correction fluid, permanent markers, dry-erase markers, fabric protecting sprays
- *Health and Beauty Supplies:* Nail polish, nail polish remover, deodorant, hairspray
- *Wood Shop Supplies:* Varnish, paint, stain, contact cement

Nitrous oxide is most often used by dentists to make patients less nervous. Known as laughing gas, nitrous oxide has a long history of abuse as an inhaled drug. Usually packaged in tanks and inhaled through plastic masks, it is easy and legal to obtain. In fact, the gas is used to make the product spray in canned whipped cream, and it is most often abused in this form.

Butane is normally used as the flammable fluid in cigarette lighters. It is sold in tobacco shops and many convenience stores, so it is cheap and easy for anyone to purchase.

Propane is best known as the fuel used to light gas barbeque grills. Many gas stations and hardware stores carry it and sell it to the public in small tanks.

Most people know helium as the gas that keeps party balloons—and even some balloons large enough to carry people or weather equipment—afloat. It is obtained in tanks through party shops and rental stores. Some of these establishments only sell the tanks to people over age 18.

Ether, one of the first general anesthetics, is not widely used today. Those who use it as an inhalant generally get it (or steal it) from research laboratories or other scientific facilities. It is now rarely sold to the public.

Chloroform is another early anesthetic. It is easy to obtain, especially over the Internet. Another gas, halothane, is a common inhaled anesthetic. It is available in liquid form and is most often sold in dark-colored bottles because light can cause the chemical structure of the gas to break down.

Solvents, Aerosols, and Adhesives

Solvents are found in a wide variety of everyday household products that can be purchased at almost any

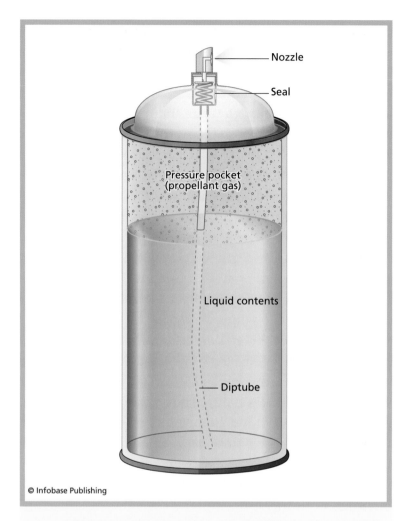

© Infobase Publishing

In a compressed gas aerosol can, high-pressure propellant gas drives the liquid in the can up the diptube and through the nozzle when the nozzle is pressed down.

grocery store or hardware store. These products include paint thinner, fire extinguishers, gasoline, nail polish remover, correction fluid, felt-tip markers, shellac, ammonia, shoe polish spray, dry-cleaning fluids, glue, degreasers, and electronic contact cleaners.

Aerosol cans are self-pressurized and dispense liquids, gases, and other substances, such as hair mousse. Aerosol cans contain two liquid substances: the product and a propellant. The propellant, which is in the form of a gas under normal pressure, becomes a liquid when subjected to the high pressure inside the can. When you press down on the nozzle, releasing some of the pressure, a bit of the propellant turns back into gas and comes out of the nozzle, carrying with it some of the product in the form of droplets. Substance abusers can inhale the gas contained in the can to get high.

Inhalant abusers also use common household adhesive products, such as model airplane glue, rubber cement, and contact cement, to get high.

Nitrites

Nitrites are a special category of inhalants. Most other inhalants act on the central nervous system. Nitrites work on the blood vessels. They dilate blood vessels, opening them so blood flows more easily. Nitrites are used in medicine to treat chest pain in people with heart disease. Unlike the vast majority of inhalants, most nitrites have been banned by the Consumer Product Safety Commission. Nonetheless, they are still available, especially online. They are sold in small bottles, often with labels reading "leather cleaner" or "video head cleaner."

Nitrites include amyl nitrite, butyl nitrite, and cyclohexyl nitrite. When used as inhalant drugs, nitrites are often referred to as "poppers." Amyl nitrite is packaged in small glass or plastic containers covered with fabric. A container is broken to release the fumes, which are then inhaled. Butyl nitrite is usually packaged in small brown vials and sold at nightclubs. Cyclohexyl nitrite is found in air freshening sprays.

STREET NAMES FOR INHALANTS

Aimies (amyl nitrite)

Air blast

Ames (amyl nitrite)

Amys (amyl nitrite)

Aroma of men (butyl nitrite)

Bagging (using inhalants)

Bang

Bolt (butyl nitrite)

Boppers (amyl nitrite)

Bullet (butyl nitrite)

Buzz bomb (nitrous oxide)

Chroming (using
  inhalants)

Climax (butyl nitrite)

Discorama (inhalant use)

Glading (inhalant use)

Gluey (an inhalant user)

Hardware

Heart-on

Highball

Hippie crack

Honey oil

Huffing (inhalant use)

Kick

Laughing gas (nitrous oxide)

Locker room (butyl nitrite)

Medusa

Moon gas

Oz

Pearls (amyl nitrite)

Poor man's pot

Poppers (amyl
  and butyl nitrite)

Quicksilver (butyl
  nitrite)

Rush (butyl nitrite)

Rush snappers
  (butyl nitrite)

Satan's secret

Shoot the breeze
  (nitrous oxide)

Snappers (butyl nitrite)

Snorting (using
  inhalants)

Snotballs
  (rubber cement
  rolled into balls,
  burned, and
  inhaled)

Spray

Texas shoeshine

Thrust (butyl nitrite)

Toilet water

Tolly (toluene)

Toncho (octane booster)

Whippets (nitrous oxide)

Whiteout
  (correction fluids)

THE CHEMICAL MAKEUP OF INHALANTS

Most inhalants, by definition, are made up of potentially hazardous chemicals. Perhaps the best-known ingredient in inhalants is toluene. Found in gasoline, paint removers, and correction fluid, it is historically the most commonly abused inhaled chemical. The body's organs easily absorb toluene. It does not simply move through the bloodstream as many other drugs do. Soon after inhaling a substance that contains toluene, a person has a level of toluene in his or her brain that is 10 times higher than the level in the blood. Because it is stored for relatively long periods in many body organs, toluene can cause brain damage and problems with the liver and kidneys.

Butane and propane—the flammable chemicals found in hairspray, air fresheners, fuel for gas grills and some types of automobiles, and lighter fluid—can cause immediate and sometimes lethal effects. Sold in pressurized liquid form, they can injure the heart and cause sudden sniffing death syndrome. In addition, because they are so flammable, these gases have caused severe burns when people inhaled them while smoking cigarettes or other drugs.

Benzene is a component of gasoline. When inhaled, benzene can injure the bone marrow, weaken the **immune system**, and damage the reproductive system. Inhaling benzene can increase a user's risk of developing **leukemia**.

Freon is used as a coolant in refrigerators and in aerosol cans. When inhaled, Freon can rupture air sacs in the lungs. Freon can cool the lungs so quickly and dramatically that people have died from inhaling it. Freon also can freeze the skin when the container is held too close to the body.

Trichloroethylene is a chemical found in degreasers and stain removers, as well as **antifreeze** and some sealants, glues, and paints. Used occasionally as a general anesthetic, it is one of the most common chemicals found in household and workplace products. Like butane and propane, it is associated with sudden sniffing death syndrome and linked to long-term problems such as **cirrhosis** of the liver, reproductive complications, and damage to vision and hearing.

The chemical compounds found in nitrites can cause the immune system to break down. They also can damage red blood cells. Nitrites can disturb the heart's rhythm, which has led to deaths. Nitrites may also be linked to an increase in risky sexual behavior that may expose users to **HIV** infection.

Methylene chloride is a chemical that is often found in paint thinners and degreasers, as well as **pesticide** sprays and some **lubricants**. When it enters the body, methylene chloride is converted into carbon monoxide and chloride. Carbon monoxide reduces the power of red blood cells to carry oxygen. It does this by taking the place of oxygen and carbon dioxide in red blood cells, so the oxygen someone is breathing cannot bind to the blood cells anymore. Eventually, carbon monoxide takes over and the body can't take in enough oxygen to stay alive. Methylene chloride can cause changes in the heart that can be fatal.

Nitrous oxide can cause death when it is inhaled in excessive quantities. It shuts off the brain's oxygen supply. Nitrous oxide also can produce **blackouts**, limb spasms, and blood pressure changes, and can slow the heartbeat to dangerously low levels.

WHAT MAKES INHALANTS SO POPULAR?

Inhalants are easily available and almost all of them are legal to buy—although it *is illegal* to abuse them. Inhalants are also very cheap, especially compared with other recreational drugs that must be obtained illicitly through drug dealers. Many inhalants, such as correction fluid, butane for lighters, and nail polish remover, cost less than two dollars. And typically, young people don't have to buy these products themselves—they just take them from around the house.

INHALABLE ALCOHOL

Many young people use inhalants as a substitute for alcohol, which can be harder to get than most inhaled products. Yet, now alcohol is being sold as an inhalant in some

Alcohol Without Liquid is a somewhat popular method of alcohol consumption in the United Kingdom. The method, which separates alcohol from its original form and turns it into a gas that can be inhaled, was introduced to Americans in 2004.

Inhalants produce an instant high that usually lasts for around 5 to 15 minutes. The immediate effects appeal to young people. Many would rather not wait the 30 minutes or longer that it can take for some drugs to kick in. The short-term high is another appealing factor. Kids can quickly get high in their bedroom, bathroom,

parts of the world. In 2004, a company called Alcohol Without Liquid (AWOL) introduced a machine that allows people to inhale shots of vaporized liquor mixed with oxygen. According to the manufacturer, inhaling alcohol produces the same intoxicated state as drinking alcohol. But inhaling alcohol doesn't cause **hangovers** because the alcohol never reaches the digestive system. It goes into the lungs, and then straight to the bloodstream.

The AWOL machine can be purchased for approximately $3,500. Some people have spoken out against the product, arguing that even underage teens could purchase it. Those in favor of AWOL, however, emphasize that the machine does not come with a supply of alcohol. Whoever purchases the machine still has to buy liquor to use with it. In theory, this should prevent teens from using the machine to get high. Still, there is an ongoing debate over whether the AWOL system should be prohibited. It remains to be seen whether inhaled alcohol will become as popular as liquid alcohol.

or even in the hallway at school between classes. Within a few minutes, they will no longer be intoxicated, so they (often incorrectly) believe they can function without changing their everyday lives or having others notice their drug usage.

Inhalants are especially popular among young people because their abuse is difficult for parents and other authority figures to detect. Drug-sniffing dogs don't search for inhalants, and it's easy to overlook their disappearance at home. They can also be kept in plain sight, with no one but the user realizing that they are being abused. Although specialized blood tests can detect the use of inhalants, the tests are costly and are rarely used.

INHALANTS AS GATEWAY DRUGS

Some inhalant abusers will experiment with any type of substance. A few, however, have a particular preference and will go out of their way to get that product. Although certain inhalants are more popular than others because they are easier to get, the 2001 Texas School Survey of Substance Abuse found that people of different age groups tend to choose different inhalants. Whereas elementary schoolchildren tend to use correction fluid and glue, high school students often use spray paint, gasoline, nitrous oxide, poppers, and paint thinner. There also are inhalant "fads": Certain types of inhalants, such as air conditioning coolant or silver and gold spray paints, will be popular for a while, before being replaced by a new substance. Often, though, young inhalant abusers don't just go from one inhalant to another. Instead, many turn to other drugs, frequently illegal ones such as marijuana, cocaine, or heroin. Inhalants are considered "gateway drugs"—substances that encourage people to experiment with illicit, highly addictive drugs.

4

Inhalants' Effects on the Body

Inhalants produce a quick high that feels similar to alcohol intoxication. The user becomes slightly excited at first, and then grows somewhat drowsy, lightheaded, and less socially inhibited. The person's coordination and judgment become impaired, making him or her prone to accidents and preventing the person from driving safely. These effects, which can begin as soon as two seconds after inhaling a chemical product, occur because inhalants act on many different parts of the brain and body.

SHORT-TERM EFFECTS OF INHALANTS

With the exception of nitrites, inhalants are **depressants**. That means that their short-term effects are similar to those seen with marijuana or alcohol use.

45

How they affect any particular person varies somewhat, based on the individual's size, weight, and general health; mood at the time of inhaling the drug; whether the person has eaten recently; whether the person has been using other drugs; and how much of the chemical substance the person has inhaled.

An inhaled chemical enters the bloodstream through the lungs, making its effects kick in much faster than those of alcohol or drugs in pill form. Any ingested drugs must go through the body's digestive system first before reaching the bloodstream, and then ultimately arriving at the brain.

The person who has used an inhalant may experience heart **palpitations**, dizziness, headache, and breathing trouble. Some users have muscle weakness, abdominal pain, mood swings, tingling or numbness in their hands and feet, hearing loss, nausea, and fatigue. In addition to feeling drunk or high, the person may become **belligerent** or exhibit violent behavior, which is a result of the impaired judgment that inhalants can produce. The user's speech may become slurred, and his or her reflexes may slow down considerably. Inhalant users may become **apathetic** and may experience hallucinations.

Even though most inhalants are depressants, many users feel a sense of euphoria after taking them. In some cases, users feel a mild excitement. In others, they become agitated and can't sit still. More commonly, they become relaxed, and laugh a lot. Users' behavior may change dramatically. They may take risks that they normally wouldn't take. They may get into fights, have unprotected sex, or have accidents that injure themselves or others. Some users become **paranoid**, thinking people are pursuing them. They may be terrified as they try to escape from these people.

Bad breath is a common side effect of inhalant use. It comes from the strong smell of chemicals that linger in the mouth after inhalation. Some users experience flu-like symptoms, such as coughing, sneezing, a runny nose, or glazed eyes. Sometimes, a user will develop nosebleeds after inhaling chemicals. Many people get sores on their mouths or noses.

Soon after the initial effects of the inhalant wear off, the user may experience the same type of symptoms seen with alcohol-related hangovers. The headaches, nausea, and dizziness may last for an entire day or even longer.

Some inhaled chemicals are associated with unique symptoms and dangers. Toluene, for instance, can make the user feel giddy, confused, or delirious. Toluene also can cause severe nausea and vomiting. Butane and propane are linked with burn injuries, because many users light cigarettes or smoke other drugs soon after inhaling these gases. This can cause the residue on or in their mouths and noses to ignite. Freon often causes severe freezing burns on the skin, along with breathing problems that can lead to death.

Short-term Effects of Nitrites

Nitrites, unlike other inhalants, are not depressants. They are **stimulants** that affect the **circulatory system**. When they are inhaled, nitrites increase the heart rate, widen the blood vessels, and make the user feel warm and excited—an unusual sensation that may last for several minutes. Nitrite users may also experience flushing of the skin, headaches, and dizziness.

Most inhalants are abused because they produce a relaxed, mellow feeling. Nitrites are used for a different purpose. Many people believe the drugs give them extra energy and enhance sexual pleasure. A significant number of nitrite users are homosexual men who think the

THE LINK BETWEEN NITRITES AND AIDS

Nitrites have been used to treat chest pain since the mid-1800s. By the 1980s, they were being used widely as a recreational drug. Amyl nitrite is often called "poppers" because of the sound the capsules make when they are broken before being inhaled. This drug was used primarily by homosexual men who believe the drug enhances sexual pleasure and performance. When the first cases of AIDS (acquired immunodeficiency syndrome) began to appear in the early 1980s, scientists wondered if nitrites might be linked in some way to the disease. In fact, some early investigators thought that poppers might actually be the cause of AIDS. Although further research showed that nitrites did not cause AIDS (which is caused by HIV, the human immunodeficiency virus), over the past two decades, a link has been found between nitrites and the tendency to become HIV positive and develop AIDS.

There are a few possibilities that have been offered to try to explain how nitrites may be linked to AIDS. First, it is believed that the high produced by nitrites may make people more likely to take part in risky sexual behavior, including unprotected intercourse, which is one of the most common ways to spread HIV. The second hypothesis relates to the fact that nitrites are known to weaken the immune system. Someone with a weak immune system is more likely to become infected if he or she is exposed to HIV than a healthy person.

drugs enhance sexual performance. Studies also show that men who abuse nitrites are at higher risk for becoming HIV positive.

LONG-TERM EFFECTS OF INHALANTS

People who use inhalants over a long period of time tend to suffer a wide range of physical and mental problems. Many lose significant, even dangerous, amounts of weight. Some experience muscle weakness and are clumsy. They can be irritable and depressed. Users may become confused and forgetful and have trouble thinking clearly or demonstrating logic. Some have tremors, and a few become hostile.

Damage to the Brain Caused by Inhalants

Long-term use of inhalants can cause irreversible brain damage. Inhalants affect several different areas of the brain. This means they can cause different types of psychological problems. They also can cause problems with the senses (seeing, hearing, tasting, smelling, and touching). Some inhalants are believed to damage the **myelin sheath**—a membrane that surrounds and protects **neurons** (brain cells). When this membrane is damaged, the cells can die.

The **cerebral cortex**, found toward the front of the brain, can be heavily affected by inhalants. When neurons die in this area of a person's brain, he or she may experience hallucinations, learning disabilities, dramatic changes in personality, and problems with memory.

Inhalants also damage the **cerebellum**, in the lower back part of the brain. The cerebellum is responsible for coordinating movements and controlling balance. Damage here can cause slurred speech, lack of coordination, and uncontrollable shaking of the arms and legs.

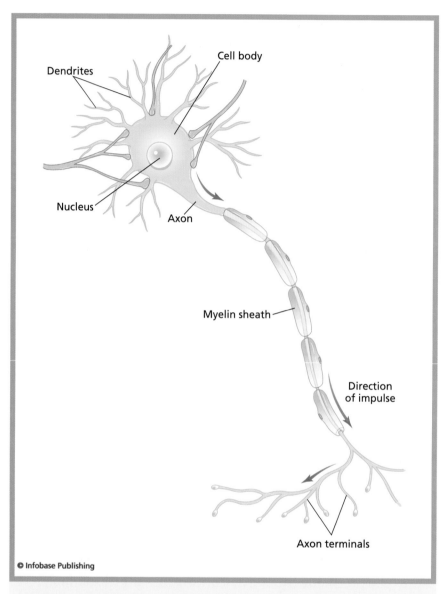

Dendrites

Cell body

Nucleus

Axon

Myelin sheath

Direction of impulse

Axon terminals

© Infobase Publishing

A neuron consists of a cell body, axon, and dendrites. The cell body contains a nucleus, which is the control center of the neuron. Axons carry nerve impulses away from the cell body. They are often wrapped in myelin, which helps increase the speed of impulse transmission. Dendrites receive nerve impulses from adjacent neurons.

Certain inhalants can cause specific types of damage to other parts of the brain. For example, toluene is known to damage the ophthalmic nerve, which is related to vision. This can cause abusers to have vision problems.

Damage to the Body Caused by Inhalants

Using inhalants over long periods of time can damage various parts of the body. Heavy doses of inhalants can lead to breathing problems, as well as problems with the heart's rhythm. Organic solvents may be the most physically dangerous inhalants. They act as poisons inside the body, breaking down cells and getting absorbed by the liver and kidneys. Inhalants can produce excessive fatty tissue in the liver, which can damage that organ. Inhalants can destroy the kidneys' ability to regulate the amount of acid in the bloodstream and also can produce **kidney stones**. Over time, inhalants can cause enough damage to make the liver and kidneys— and many other organs—fail.

Chronic inhalant use can lead to muscle **wasting**, decreased strength, and reduced muscle tone. The bone marrow can be damaged, sometimes leading to leukemia. Hearing loss also can occur; inhalants damage the cells that carry sounds to the brain. Many users also develop a rash around the nose and mouth known as "glue-sniffer's rash."

Certain inhalants, including methylene chloride (found in paint thinner) and nitrites, affect the blood's ability to carry oxygen. The lungs are at particular risk, because inhalants travel there first. The heart also is at risk. Most inhalants tend to slow down the heart to dangerous levels, while others—especially nitrites—speed it up. When the heart's rhythm becomes abnormal, the person is at risk of **cardiac arrest** and death.

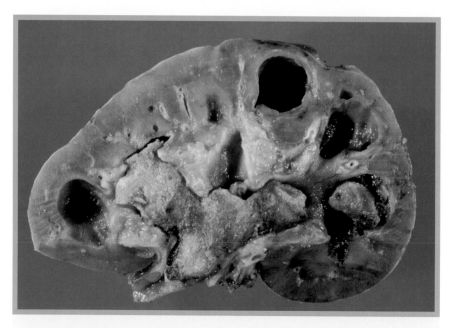

Using inhalants over a long period of time can cause kidney stones to form in the body. A kidney stone is a solid mass, usually made of calcium and other substances in crystal form, that moves from the kidney to the groin area. Kidney stones are extremely painful. This image shows a large kidney stone in the lower center of the kidney's pelvic region, as well as smaller stones on the right and in the cavities of the kidney.

Nitrous oxide, the popular inhalant found in whipped cream cans, causes damage to the **peripheral nerves**. Long-term use produces symptoms that include numbness or tingling in the arms, hands, legs, and feet. In some cases, nitrous oxide can paralyze the body.

Another inhalant, toluene, has many negative effects on the body. Toluene can:

- Damage **chromosomes**
- Injure eggs and sperm
- Lead to premature birth or the death of a fetus

- Cause birth defects
- Cause long-term problems after a child is born

In some cases, the baby even suffers **withdrawal** from inhalant drugs because of the mother's inhalant abuse during pregnancy.

Nitrites also cause specific damage to the body. When used over a long period of time, nitrites raise the pressure of the fluid in the eyes. This can lead to **glaucoma** and even blindness. Even if vision problems don't occur, habitual use of nitrites can produce pounding headaches that last for long periods.

OTHER RISKS OF INHALANT USE
Sudden Sniffing Death Syndrome

There are some instant and sometimes fatal consequences to using inhalants. What many young users don't realize is that it is possible to die the very first time you try an inhalant. This phenomenon is called sudden sniffing death syndrome (SSDS). It's the most common cause of death among inhalant abusers. Studies show that 22% of people who die of SSDS had never tried inhalants before.

Sudden sniffing death syndrome happens when the inhalant user is startled while huffing. Examples of this include when a young person is inhaling and his or her parents walk into the room unexpectedly, and when the user is startled by a hallucination caused by the inhalant itself.

When a person gets surprised, a hormone called epinephrine (also known as adrenaline) surges through the body. Epinephrine prepares the body to face a challenge. It increases the amount of energy available. It also increases the heart rate and blood pressure. When an inhalant is in the bloodstream, the heart becomes more

THE DIFFERENT WAYS INHALANTS CAN KILL

In addition to the danger of sudden sniffing death syndrome, inhalants can cause death in a number of other ways. These include:

- *Allergies:* Some people are allergic to certain inhalants. Someone who doesn't realize he or she has such an allergy may suffer **anaphylactic shock** after ingesting the substance. This often is fatal.
- *Asphyxiation:* When a person repeatedly inhales a chemical, the fumes accumulate in the lungs. This leaves little room for oxygen and can cause breathing difficulties and death.
- *Choking:* Because many inhalants cause nausea and vomiting, users may throw up while huffing and can choke to death on their own vomit.
- *Coma:* Over time, inhalant abuse kills brain cells. This causes memory and movement problems. If enough brain cells die, the brain may shut down completely. This leads to a **coma** that may be irreversible.

sensitive to epinephrine. If epinephrine is released, the heart beats in a rapid, irregular rhythm. This **arrhythmia** can kill the inhalant user in seconds.

Other Risks of Inhalant Use

The possibility of dying while abusing inhalants isn't the only risk users face. While high on inhaled drugs,

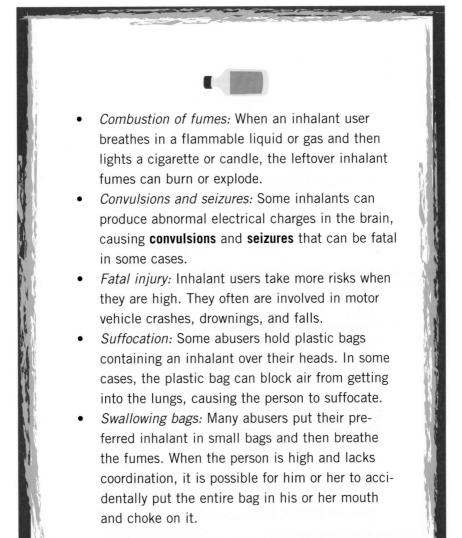

- *Combustion of fumes:* When an inhalant user breathes in a flammable liquid or gas and then lights a cigarette or candle, the leftover inhalant fumes can burn or explode.
- *Convulsions and seizures:* Some inhalants can produce abnormal electrical charges in the brain, causing **convulsions** and **seizures** that can be fatal in some cases.
- *Fatal injury:* Inhalant users take more risks when they are high. They often are involved in motor vehicle crashes, drownings, and falls.
- *Suffocation:* Some abusers hold plastic bags containing an inhalant over their heads. In some cases, the plastic bag can block air from getting into the lungs, causing the person to suffocate.
- *Swallowing bags:* Many abusers put their preferred inhalant in small bags and then breathe the fumes. When the person is high and lacks coordination, it is possible for him or her to accidentally put the entire bag in his or her mouth and choke on it.

people lose their ability to reason. They are more likely to take chances that can lead to accidents, such as nearly drowning or motor vehicle incidents.

This lack of judgment also puts the user at risk of sex abuse and other sex-related dangers. Those who are high on inhalants make easy targets for sexual predators. In addition, inhalant abusers are more likely to get sexually transmitted diseases (STDs). That's because people high on inhalants are more likely to have unprotected sex.

Suicide is yet another risk of inhalant abuse. Many young people abuse inhalants to help them deal with stress, depression, or other problems. As a result, they don't learn healthy ways to handle life's stresses. This can lead to long-term mental health problems and suicidal thoughts. In some cases, people impulsively decide to kill themselves while they are high on inhalants. Others become depressed as their inhalant high wears off and may choose to commit suicide. Suicide also is linked with inhalant abuse because most chronic abusers already have serious emotional or psychological problems *before* they begin huffing.

Finally, people who use inhalants can get addicted. When someone uses a particular drug over a period of time, the body begins to need more of it to achieve the same high the person achieved the first time they took the drug. This is known as **tolerance**. Over time, the body not only needs more of the drug to get high, but also starts needing the drug just to feel normal. This is addiction. Once someone is addicted to inhalants and begins to use them more often, he or she increases the risk of all the physical problems that inhalants can cause—including death.

No one knows for certain exactly how many people die each year as a result of inhalant abuse. Many young people lie about their use of inhalants. Most drug tests don't check for inhalants. Many of the deaths actually caused by inhalants are reported instead as motor vehicle accidents, drownings, or suffocations. What we do know is that the number of emergency room visits related to inhalants has been growing over the past several years. In 2005, almost 5,000 U.S. hospital visits were linked with inhalant use, including the visits by more than 600 people who attempted suicide while high on inhalants.

5

Why People Use Inhalants

People tend to use inhalants for the same reasons they use other kinds of drugs. Some are looking for pleasurable feelings. Others use inhalants to try to dull physical or psychological pain. Young people often have specific reasons for using inhalants that differ from the reasons adults have. Young people may be interested in challenging the rules and values of their parents and teachers, or they may be trying to get someone to pay attention to them. Some are just curious and want to know what it feels like. And others use inhalant drugs because their friends are doing it and they want to fit in.

WHY GET HIGH?

A study funded by the National Institute on Drug Abuse (NIDA) asked 285 young people in juvenile correction facilities to describe the good and bad things about inhalants. Almost 61% said that they experienced euphoria, feeling happy, high, and free from worries. Other young

INHALANT ABUSE IS INCREASING AMONG GIRLS

In March 2007, a national news report showed that inhalant abuse is increasing among girls. Research done by the Substance Abuse and Mental Health Services Administration (SAMHSA) indicated that more than 600,000 young people began to use inhalants in 2005. Of those new users, 268,000 were boys and 337,000 were girls. The study also showed that girls begin to use inhalants at much younger ages than boys do. Peer pressure is a particularly strong factor in leading girls to try inhalants. According to Wayne Beatty, the safe schools program administrator for the Natrona County School District in Wyoming, the news was not a big surprise. Beatty said that he had worked with three girls over the previous six months. Each had been caught using inhalants and was forced by a court to undergo drug counseling. One of the most common inhalants being used in the Natrona County area was canned air, the type used to clean the crevices of keyboards and electronics. Using these products as inhalant drugs is called "dusting." Two of the girls had been caught shoplifting canned air.

This new evidence uncovered by the SAMHSA study suggests that parents and teachers need to talk to girls about the dangers of inhalant use early in the preteen years, before the girls actually begin to experiment with inhalants.

people said they felt relaxed or as if they were detached from their bodies, floating in the air instead of being grounded in the physical world. Almost one-third said that they felt effects relating to social behavior: They became more talkative or felt sexually aroused. A smaller number (around 8%) said that their emotions were dulled, making them feel less worried or depressed.

Many teens, however, reported unpleasant effects after using inhalants. About 39% experienced hallucinations. More than 28% had memory problems. Some people lost consciousness and others had blackouts. More than 25% of users became dizzy or lightheaded, while 7% became depressed or experienced an aftertaste or unpleasant odor after using inhalants. More than 32% said that they suffered other symptoms, such as headaches, nausea, and a loss of coordination.

WHY DO YOUNG PEOPLE USE INHALANTS?

Most adults think that inhalants produce an unpleasant high. In contrast, children and young adults enjoy the effects because inhalants make users feel dizzy and disoriented. Many children spin around in circles on purpose, or go on amusement park rides such as roller coasters, to produce this feeling. This may be why children and young adults like inhalants and most adults don't.

Young people are also drawn to inhalants for other reasons. As many as 1,500 products can be used as inhalant drugs, and they all are available for legitimate household, commercial, and industrial uses. Just about every household has several of these products on hand.

Cost is another reason inhalants are so popular among preteens and young adults. Because so many inhalable products can be found in the average household, kids often can get them for free. Even if they have to buy them, most inhalants are inexpensive and legal for anyone to buy in a store. There are no age restrictions or medical prescriptions needed.

Also, most inhaled drugs don't require **parapher-nalia**, such as pipes and rolling papers. Almost all inhalants can be used alone or with common items such as cloth or plastic bags.

Many young people abuse inhalants because, unlike most other drugs, they can be used anywhere. The products are easy to explain if the user is caught with them. Inhalants don't really need to be hidden. The products can "hide in plain sight." Studies show that most adults either don't know about inhalant abuse, or don't believe that their children could be using inhalants. This makes it even easier for kids to get away with abusing inhalants.

Inhalants also are popular because few children and teens recognize the dangers. Because these products are readily available and legal, people think they can't cause any real harm. Inhalant abuse is not as widely reported as the use of illegal drugs such as cocaine and Ecstasy. Many young users never make the connection between inhalants and the dangers of drug use. Many teens think that reports of the dangers of inhalant use are urban legends.

Perhaps the most common reason young people start using inhalants is peer pressure. Almost all inhalant abuse is done in groups. People usually don't use inhalants alone until they've developed a habit.

Peer pressure causes young people to do things they wouldn't usually do. For example, there have been widespread reports of adolescents huffing in groups and competing to see who can fall into unconsciousness first. Of course, the results of such events can be deadly as large amounts may easily be inhaled quickly with no regard for how sick users are feeling.

THE LINK BETWEEN INHALANT USE AND PSYCHOLOGICAL PROBLEMS

Another common reason for using inhalants is depression. People with depression, anxiety, or other psychological problems are more likely to become dependent on inhalants. These disorders also make people more likely to try inhalants in the first place. They may be seeking a way to ease the emotional distress they are feeling.

In 2004, the National Institute on Drug Abuse completed a study. The research showed that some young people were more likely to start using inhalants than others. They included:

- Those who started using inhalants by age 13 or 14
- Those who had been in foster care
- Those who had been treated for any type of mental health problem
- Those who already abused or were addicted to at least two other drugs

Emotional problems can make teens more likely to try inhalants, and to keep using them. The more serious the emotional problem is, the more heavily involved with inhalant abuse the person may become. This is because the person is more likely to feel better when he or she uses inhalants.

PATTERNS OF INHALANT USAGE

In the United States, inhalants have been used since at least the 1800s. Today, inhalants are perhaps more popular than ever. Many of the young adults who abuse inhalants are from the middle- and upper-middle classes. But most of these users tend to stop using inhalants by the time they reach their late teens or early twenties. In poor communities, however, many inhalant users continue to abuse inhalants as adults.

In other parts of the world, inhalant use is almost exclusively done by the poor and the homeless. Sniffing dung out of plastic bags or metal tins is a particular problem in Southeast Asian countries such as Malaysia and

INHALANTS IN POPULAR CULTURE

Inhalant use, like the use of many other recreational drugs, has been portrayed in several movies and works of literature that make up American popular culture.

Singer Kurt Cobain sang a line about inhaling glue in a Nirvana song called "Dumb." Cobain, who had a history of depression and painful stomach problems, also used marijuana and heroin, among other drugs.

Thailand. Glue sniffing is approaching epidemic levels in parts of South and Central America. In the 1980s in Russia and Eastern Europe, laws were passed to prevent sailors from drinking too much alcohol. Since then, gasoline sniffing among sailors has been common.

Even though inhalants are common, some people have specific reasons for avoiding them. Some teens

The Ramones, a punk band that reached the height of their popularity in the 1980s, had a hit with their song "Now I Wanna Sniff Some Glue." In 1998, the band Primus sang "Lacquer Head," a tune about teens using inhalants to get high.

Journalist Hunter S. Thompson's semiautobiographical novel *Fear and Loathing in Las Vegas* was made into a film starring Johnny Depp in 1998. The novel includes scenes of the lead characters inhaling diethyl ether. In the 1996 movie *Citizen Ruth,* the title character inhales patio sealant out of a paper bag.

Some real-life pop culture icons were also known to abuse inhalants. Kurt Cobain, lead singer of Nirvana, was said to have inhaled the gas from shaving cream cans. Janis Joplin, the 1960s singer best known for the songs "Me and Bobby McGee" and "Piece of My Heart," also supposedly used inhalants. Both singers also had well-documented histories with other drugs. Sadly, Cobain committed suicide in 1994, while Joplin died of a heroin overdose in 1970.

Glue sniffing has become a major problem among children in parts of the Central American country of El Salvador. This 2003 image shows a sleeping Jose Arnoldo, a young boy who regularly sniffs glue with his friends and falls into a deep sleep. Government programs work to break the children's addictions, keep them healthy, and send them to school.

think that inhalants are "gutter drugs"—the kind of drugs that only very poor people or people who are perceived as low-class "junkies" take because they don't cost a lot of money. Some teens notice that inhalants aren't often shown in the media as glamorous to use. Others dislike the bad smell that frequently lingers on inhalant abusers. Some teens feel that parents, authority figures, and peers would disapprove. Some teens don't enjoy the high that inhalants produce, and increasing numbers of young people are becoming more aware of the dangers of inhalants, leading them to stay away from the drugs.

6

Abuse and Addiction

When Megan was 12, she was sexually assaulted. She went to counseling after the attack, but it didn't completely help. By the time she turned 13, she had found a way to make herself feel better. She started huffing. Within a few months, she was abusing inhalants—mostly air freshening sprays—every day. She couldn't stop doing it. Megan had become addicted.

Megan's parents had no idea that their daughter had a problem with drugs. "It never even crossed my mind," her mother said. One of Megan's teachers mentioned that Megan seemed to have lost some weight. This is one of many signs of possible drug use. But Megan's parents still couldn't believe there was anything wrong.

Eventually, Megan's mom became curious enough to do a little snooping. When she went through Megan's things, she found notes written by Megan and her friends that mentioned inhalant use. Megan's parents took her to a drug counselor. The counseling didn't go well. A week after Megan's first session, she had a fight with her brother and swallowed pills in an attempt to commit suicide. She survived, but her parents realized that they had to send her to rehab.

For the first three weeks of rehab, Megan was bitter and angry with her parents for forcing her to stop using inhalants. Then she had a change of heart. She realized how dangerous inhalants were, both to her health and to her relationship with her family. Although Megan admits that she sometimes feels peer pressure to use inhalants again, she has stayed clean. She has given talks in front of her church group about inhalants and how addictive they can be.

Megan was lucky. She survived the risk of immediate death while huffing. She beat her addiction and has gone on to live a healthier life. Not all inhalant addicts can say the same.

WHAT IS ADDICTION?

People can become addicted to any drug. The first time a person uses a drug, the high usually happens quickly. After that first time, the body starts to get used to the drug. Over time, it takes more of the drug to achieve the same high the person felt that first time.

As the body builds up a tolerance, it starts to need the drug just to feel normal. This is physical addiction. Without enough of the drug, the user experiences unpleasant withdrawal symptoms. These include headache, nausea, vomiting, and irritability. In many ways, withdrawal feels like being sick.

SIGNS THAT SOMEONE MAY BE USING INHALANTS

Here are some signs of inhalant abuse:

- Changes in school performance and declining grades
- Slurred speech
- Empty aerosol cans, balloons, or rags with a chemical smell around the house
- Changes in mood, including irritability or excitability
- Stains or evidence of paint on the hands or face
- Sores or rashes around the mouth and nose
- Problems with physical coordination
- Hanging around with new friends
- Changes in hobbies or interests
- A dazed look
- Loss of appetite
- Lethargy
- Frequent headaches
- A chemical smell on the person's clothing or breath

In addition to physical addiction, a drug user may become psychologically addicted. In this case, the person's craving for the drug is not physical, but mental. The user feels an overwhelming desire to have the drug. He or she may associate using the drug with pleasant experiences. People who are addicted, either physically or psychologically, have little control over whether they use the drug. They feel as if they *have* to have it.

INHALANTS AND CRIME

Although most inhalants are legal to own and easy to get, there is still a relationship between inhalant use and crime.

One study involved inhalant abusers in Albuquerque, New Mexico. Researchers looked at the arrest records of 100 juvenile delinquents who were chronic inhalant users. They were more likely than nonusers to face arrest for almost every kind of criminal activity, including violent offenses.

A similar study analyzed a sample of more than 13,000 students in grades 7 through 12, breaking them into five groups: chronic inhalant users, those who experiment with inhalants, chronic users of other drugs, those who experiment with other drugs, and those who don't use drugs or inhalants. Inhalant users and inhalant experimenters in grades 9–12 were involved in more criminal activity than the users of other drugs and those who experiment with other drugs. The study suggested that inhalant abuse is somehow different from the abuse of other drugs, and that it is more closely linked to criminal behavior and delinquency.

According to a 2002 study by the Texas Commission on Alcohol and Drug Abuse, many young adults who abuse inhalants have problems with **truancy** and may do poorly in school. They are also more likely to drop out of school than nonusers.

A study in the *Journal of Substance Abuse* found that inhalant abusers are more likely to drink alcohol frequently and to binge drink. Inhalant abusers also have higher rates of other drug abuse and tobacco use while in college.

THE SIGNS OF ADDICTION

Many addicts can hide their problem from the people around them. But certain signs suggest that someone has a problem with drugs. Drug users may gain or lose substantial amounts of weight. They may begin to hang around with a different group of friends. They may lose interest in activities that they once enjoyed. They may seem nervous or have mood swings.

PROBLEMS CAUSED BY INHALANT ADDICTION

People who use inhalants are just as likely to become addicted as someone who uses any other addictive drug. Inhalants can be so addicting that after using them for a year, someone who sniffs glue to get high may have to inhale eight to ten tubes of plastic cement just to get the same feeling they got from one tube when they first started using.

Withdrawal symptoms usually begin just a few hours after the last time the person used an inhalant. The user may become irritable, aggressive, depressed, or **lethargic**. These symptoms can be so severe that users feel as if they need to use an inhalant just to feel better.

When inhalants are abused over a long period of time, they cause many problems, including:

- Inhalants—especially toluene—are **toxic** to the nervous system, causing brain damage.
- Sniffing gasoline can cause lead poisoning, muscle paralysis, and **dementia**.
- Nitrites can increase the risk of contracting **infectious diseases** and even cancer.
- Chronic inhalant abuse can cause **electrolyte** imbalances and kidney damage, including a form of kidney disease called glomerulonephritis.

- Many inhalant users develop liver abnormalities, which can be made worse by alcohol abuse.
- Because inhalants travel straight to the lungs, users often have lung **inflammation** and infections such as **pneumonia**.
- Benzene (found in gasoline) is toxic to the bone marrow, while other inhalants can damage the blood vessels.
- Although there is little direct evidence yet, many scientists believe that inhalant use during pregnancy can cause problems for both the mother and fetus. Some studies suggest that inhalants can cause a condition similar to **fetal alcohol syndrome**.
- Chronic inhalant users may also develop psychological or behavior problems. Many become dangerously aggressive or violent, and may even become **psychopathic**. Inhalant addicts also are likely to commit crimes.

7

Getting Help and Preventing Inhalant Use

Inhalants are one of the most widely used drugs in the United States. One in every five teens in the country has tried them. Only alcohol, marijuana, and tobacco have been used by more young people. Yet only 5% of parents think it's possible that their kids have tried inhalants. Clearly, it can be difficult to tell if someone is using inhalants.

WARNING SIGNS OF INHALANT ABUSE

The adolescent years can be a rough time, with or without drugs. Many young people become very emotional as a result of the hormonal changes they are going through. At times, it might seem like they are using drugs. However, unlike the physical and behavioral symptoms of drug use, most non-drug-related physical and behavioral problems go away within a short period of time. In addition, certain warning signs that aren't related to normal adolescent changes can point to drug use.

Physical Signs

Several physical signs often occur in people who are abusing inhalants. They include:

- Watery, glassy, or glazed-looking eyes
- Slurred or confused speech
- A lack of physical coordination
- A dizzy or dazed appearance

Some inhalant users may act like they've been drinking alcohol and seem clumsy. Many become nauseated and may not eat. This loss of appetite can lead to extreme, easily noticeable weight loss. Users may have red eyes and a runny nose, and they often develop a rash or sores around the nose and mouth. Some have frequent nosebleeds. The user's skin often takes on a pale, bluish tint. Finally, many inhalant abusers have an unusual or chemical smell on their breath and their clothes.

Behavioral Signs

When people are using inhalants, their behavior can change in dramatic ways. Some have severe mood swings or become irritable, angry, anxious, restless, or overly excitable. Young people who once did well in school may suddenly begin to have trouble. They might have problems with teachers, miss days of school, not turn in homework, or fail tests. An inhalant abuser may seem not to care about life and may be forgetful. Some have hallucinations, and others may seem afraid.

WHERE TO GET HELP

Find information and get help by contacting the following organizations:

Alliance for Consumer Education
www.inhalant.org

American Council for Drug Education
www.acde.org

Drug Abuse Resistance Education
www.dare-america.com

Join Together
www.jointogether.org

Narcotics Anonymous
www.na.org

National Inhalant Prevention Coalition
www.inhalants.com

National Institute on Drug Abuse
www.nida.nih.gov

Office of National Drug Control Policy
www.theantidrug.com

Partnership for a Drug-Free America
www.drugfree.org

StreetDrugs.org
www.streetdrugs.org

Substance Abuse and Mental Health Services Administration
www.samhsa.org

Situational Signs

People who are abusing inhalants may have specific things on their bodies or in their homes that may indicate that they are using drugs. Although it is common for some people to have paint residue on their hands, inhalant abusers often have traces of paint or other chemical products in unusual places, such as on the cheeks, nose, or lips. They may also have paint stains or other kinds of stains on their clothing.

Another sign of inhalant abuse is when people paint their fingernails with something other than nail polish—such as correction fluid or markers. Some inhalant abusers will sit in class with pens or markers held up close to their noses, so they can sniff them even during the school day. Many will frequently sniff at their sleeves, collars, or hair scrunchies made of cloth.

Inhalant abusers may keep lighters in their rooms, lockers, purses, or backpacks—even if they don't smoke. There may be cleaning products or air fresheners missing from around the user's home. Users may have rags, clothing, or empty containers hidden in closets or under their beds. There may also be spray paint cans, gasoline, or chemical-soaked cloths in places like the bedroom, where they don't normally belong.

WHAT TO DO IF SOMEONE YOU KNOW IS ABUSING INHALANTS

If you find out that a friend or family member has been abusing inhalants, there are a few steps you can take to try to help the person. First, if the person is currently under the influence of an inhalant, do not excite him or her, or start an argument. Inhalants can make some users aggressive and even violent. Stay calm and don't panic. If the person is actively huffing in your presence, do not surprise or startle him or her. An unexpected fright can lead to sudden sniffing death syndrome. Making the person overexcited also can cause hallucinations.

If you find your friend unconscious or if the person is not breathing, you should call 911 and perform **CPR** (cardiopulmonary resuscitation) until the emergency medical team arrives. If anyone else is around, find out what the person has been inhaling. If your friend was huffing alone, have someone check for signs of what he or she was using, such as aerosol or spray paint cans or rags soaked in chemicals. If the person is conscious but still high, get him or her into a room that is well ventilated and try to keep the person calm.

Maybe you haven't actually caught your friend in the act of abusing inhalants, but you suspect that the person is using them. Approach the person calmly and with a lot of caring. Many inhalant abusers will become defensive and deny that there is a problem. Teen users often become especially angry if they are accused of abusing inhalants by parents or teachers. When you talk to the person, explain that you are worried. Try not to sound like you are accusing him or her. Focus on explaining how the person's drug abuse is affecting *you*, rather than simply condemning your friend for using inhalants. Do not mention rumors or things you have heard from other people about your friend's drug use. Stick to discussing things you have witnessed personally.

Once you have confirmed that the person has a problem, it is important to look for professional help. You could talk with a school guidance counselor or nurse, a family physician, or another health-care worker. These people can help the inhalant abuser find treatment.

TREATMENT FOR DRUG ADDICTION

The main purpose of drug addiction treatment is to help a person stop using the drug in question and to learn how to live without it. Addiction treatment also aims to keep new users from becoming addicted to drugs. The success of treatment programs helps to reduce these costs. According to the National Institute on Drug Abuse, illegal drug abuse costs the United States almost $200 billion each year.

Studies have shown that formal drug treatment programs fulfill a few specific aims: They help drug users stop taking drugs, prevent relapses, and change the thought patterns and behaviors that led them to start abusing drugs in the first place. The National Institute on Drug Abuse has laid out a few principles that should be part of any effective treatment program. These include the following:

- No one type of treatment will work for every person.
- Drug treatment needs to be easily available to everyone.
- The treatment should help the person with all aspects of his or her life, not just the drug abuse.
- The treatment program needs to be analyzed and changed as needed over time.
- The person needs to stay in the treatment program for a long enough time to develop new behaviors and ways of thinking.
- Counseling and other behavior-related therapies should be part of any drug treatment program.
- Drug users who also have other mental illnesses should receive treatment that addresses both the addiction and the other psychological disorders in a compatible way.

Colin Hartman poses in a storefront he uses as an art gallery in Williamsport, Pennsylvania, in 2004. Hartman struggled with an addiction to inhalants for 15 years. Now he tries to communicate the dangers of huffing to others through his artwork.

- Medication to minimize withdrawal symptoms should only be used at the start of addiction treatment; it doesn't help eliminate long-term drug use.
- Even if the person is forced into treatment against his or her will, the program can be effective.
- The program needs to monitor patients carefully to make sure they are not using drugs while they are undergoing treatment.

- Drug treatment should screen patients for infectious diseases, such as HIV/AIDS and **hepatitis**, which are often related to drug use.
- Patients may need several courses of addiction treatment if they are to remain drug free in the long term.

INHALANT ABUSE TREATMENT CAN BE HARD TO FIND

In many ways, inhalant abuse is different from other forms of drug use. For one thing, most inhalants are legal products (although it is illegal to abuse them). For another, drug tests almost never check for inhalant abuse, so it can be difficult to prove that someone is abusing inhalants.

In addition, inhalant abusers themselves tend to be different from other drug users. They frequently use more than one drug (or, at least, more than one type of inhalant). They usually have a background that includes a dysfunctional family, low self-esteem, **neurological** problems, and a history of mental health issues. All of these factors make inhalant treatment more complicated than treatment for other types of drugs.

Even though inhalants can be just as addictive—both physically and psychologically—as many other recreational drugs, there is little government funding targeted for inhalant abuse treatment. Often, the media and the public don't pay attention to the issue of inhalant use. As a result, it can be difficult to find treatment for someone who wants to stop taking inhalants. To make matters worse, many drug treatment facilities won't accept inhalant abusers, mainly because some scientists argue that traditional rehabilitation does not work for inhalant users. Some rehab facilities have personnel and programs that are capable of treating inhalant abusers. Only a small number of places are focused specifically on the treatment of these addicts.

Even so, inhalant abusers need to go through some form of **detoxification** and rehabilitation in order to overcome their drug habit. Scientists believe that it can take six weeks for heavy inhalant users to get inhalants out of their systems.

HOW IS INHALANT ABUSE TREATED?

In general, inhalant abusers require the same kind of detoxification treatment provided for alcoholics. Treatment should start by sending patients to an environment with little sensory stimulation and calmly letting them know that they are going to get better. At the start of treatment, it is important to obtain a complete history of the patient's inhalant use, because most users have experimented with multiple inhalants. It is also important to perform a thorough physical examination of the patient, including extensive blood tests, to identify any and all substances the person has been using.

A rehabilitation facility should take special precautions when admitting an inhalant abuser. Because so many household and commercial products can be abused, the facility has to be careful to make sure that any abusable products are replaced with nonsolvent, nonaerosol products.

Other drug abusers may be given medication to help them get through the unpleasant withdrawal symptoms that occur when they stop using their drug of choice. For example, heroin addicts are often treated with a drug called methadone, which comes from the same family of drugs as heroin and can help decrease the person's need for heroin. At the present time, there are no drugs to help inhalant users overcome their addiction.

It takes longer for inhalant drugs to pass through the body than it does for alcohol and many other drugs. Most inhalant treatment programs require addicts to detoxify for at least two weeks; more often, it's a full month. After this time, the inhalant abuser's mental functions begin to return to normal. However, some of the brain damage can be permanent.

Once inhalant abusers have detoxified, they can begin the long-term portion of the treatment. Since their brains are now functioning more normally, they can take part in psychotherapy and behavioral treatments that are designed to help them live without using inhalants. This part of treatment takes around six months. In many cases, recovering inhalant users need to stay in therapy for as long as two years. Relapse is also extremely common among inhalant users, so the treatment has to take steps to help patients learn other ways to relax and enjoy their free time so they don't go back to inhalant abuse.

TYPES OF TREATMENT

There are many forms of treatment available for people who are trying to kick a drug habit. The two main types are **pharmacological** (using medication to help the patient stop using drugs) and behavioral (helping the patient change the behaviors that led him or her to start using drugs). Because there are currently no approved medications available for treating inhalant abuse, most treatment for inhalant users is behavioral in focus. Regardless of the type of treatment, getting professional help is essential for overcoming an inhalant addiction. It is almost impossible to recover alone.

RECOMMENDED INHALANT ABUSE TREATMENT APPROACHES

The Substance Abuse and Mental Health Services Administration (SAMHSA) has created a set of guidelines for creating effective treatment programs for inhalant abusers. They include the following:

- Drug treatment facilities and prevention organizations should provide medical professionals with information about inhalant abuse, so they can do a better job of identifying people who are using inhalants.
- People who work in drug treatment should rigorously check into whether patients are using inhalants. Many patients are reluctant to admit to using inhalants. A detailed history and physical examination should be performed.
- Allow enough time for the inhalant abuser to detoxify completely (generally two to six weeks). Detoxification should be followed by extensive therapy (for as long as two years).
- The initial therapy sessions should be short (about 15 to 20 minutes long), since many inhalant abusers have short attention spans and have trouble with complex thinking.
- Assess the patient's **cognitive** functioning and check to see if he or she has suffered any neurological or physical damage as a result of inhalant use.

(continues on page 84)

(continued from page 83)

- Because so many people start using inhalants at very young ages, treatment needs to teach life skills and work with any neurological damage that may already have occurred.
- Include the patient's family in the treatment as much as possible, especially when the patient is a child or young adult.
- The patient should be gradually introduced to a new peer group whose members don't abuse inhalants.
- Make sure there are no products available in the treatment facility that patients might abuse if given the opportunity.
- Be sure that all staff members at the treatment facility are knowledgeable about the dangers of inhalants.
- Create a plan for treating the patient after the initial rehabilitation program is completed. If the patient is a young person, make sure the school or a private counselor is involved in the aftercare.

Behavioral therapy teaches patients ways to cope with their cravings for drugs, helps them learn how to avoid drug use and relapsing, and helps them deal with relapse if it does occur. The goal of behavioral therapy is, as the name implies, to change patients' behavior as it relates to drug use and to help them learn how to live healthier lives. There are a number of different kinds of behavioral therapy.

Cognitive-behavioral therapy deals not only with behavior but also with the way the person thinks. It helps patients learn why they use drugs in certain situations and teaches them to develop ways to avoid using drugs. Cognitive-behavioral therapy is based on the idea that the way we learn plays a major role in the habits and behaviors we develop. By learning to respond in new ways to the situations in which patients once used drugs, patients can "unlearn" their desire to take drugs and substitute healthier behaviors instead.

The main goal of cognitive-behavioral therapy is to avoid relapse. Patients learn to notice when they have drug cravings and to understand the kinds of situations, or "triggers," that make them want to use drugs. Then they learn new ways to behave in those situations. By learning to avoid high-risk situations and to deal with cravings when they happen, patients learn to live without drugs. According to the National Institute on Drug Abuse, studies show that the strategies people learn as part of cognitive-behavioral therapy remain in effect long after treatment has stopped.

Behavioral therapy uses a few specific techniques just for adolescents who are trying to beat a drug addiction. Teens are given models for proper behavior and receive praise and rewards when they achieve goals that reflect their new, drug-free lifestyle. The therapist may give the teenage patient "homework" assignments to do, where they practice the behaviors that will help them avoid using drugs.

One aspect of behavioral therapy for teens is stimulus control. The therapist helps the patient stay away from situations that are related to drug use, such as parties and raves or certain friends who still use drugs. Patients are also encouraged to take part in other behaviors, such as sports, that aren't compatible with drug abuse.

Another aspect of behavioral therapy is urge control. Teens learn to recognize the thoughts and feelings that lead them to take drugs and they learn to replace those thoughts with healthier ones.

Still another aspect of behavioral therapy is social control. The teen's family members, friends, and other people (such as teachers or coaches) get involved in helping the teen avoid drug use. Often, the teen's parents or boyfriend or girlfriend comes to the therapy sessions and help the patient complete the homework assigned by the therapist.

Like other forms of behavioral therapy, multidimensional family therapy (MDFT) teaches teenage patients to notice the aspects of their lives that influence their drug abuse. However, MDFT directly involves teens' entire families as part of the treatment. MDFT teaches how various people—including family members, friends, and the community—affect the patient and his or her drug use, and helps the whole family understand why certain situations lead the teen to use drugs. Together, the family learns ways to put an end to drug-using behavior.

As part of MDFT, the teen with the drug problem attends individual therapy sessions as well as group sessions with his or her family. In the individual meetings, the therapist and teen work on developing better decision-making and problem-solving skills. Teens also learn how to talk about how they feel, and they learn ways to deal with life's stresses. The family sessions help the whole family understand what the teen is learning in the individual sessions, so that everyone can develop better decision-making skills. In some cases, parents also attend therapy sessions of their own, where they learn specific strategies to help their child.

Because inhalant abuse often happens in groups, one of the most important aspects of therapy is to help users become part of new peer groups whose members don't use inhalants. Education is also an essential part of therapy. If young people are made more aware of the dangers of inhalants, they are less likely to try them.

TIPS FOR MAKING RECOVERY EASIER

If you or a friend is trying to stop abusing inhalants, there are a few things you can do to make sure your treatment is as effective as possible. First, inform every-one you know that you have decided to stop using drugs. If they're really your friends, your peers will understand your decision and respect it. Unfortunately, in some cases, your friends will try to talk you into con-tinuing to use inhalants. If this happens, it is important to stop hanging out with these people and try to find new friends who will be supportive of your decision to lead a healthier, drug-free life.

You should also let your family and friends know that you may need their support. Ask the people you love to be there for you when you need to talk, when you're having a hard time dealing with your cravings for inhalants, or when you have to be in a situation where you may be tempted to start using again.

Don't go to places where you know there will be drugs or alcohol. At least at the beginning of your recovery, you should also try to stay away from places and people that you associate with inhalant abuse. Try taking up new hobbies or hanging out in places, such as a gym or community center, where drug use isn't very common.

Come up with a plan for how you will handle your-self if you end up someplace where other people are

A can of aerosol dust remover offers a warning that a bitterant has been added to the contents to discourage inhalant abuse of the product.

using drugs or alcohol. Behavioral therapy will help you learn new ways to deal with cravings for inhalants and to handle being at parties or other places where people abuse drugs. If you feel like you're being tempted to start using drugs again, leave the party or ask a friend or family member to pick you up.

Remember that relapse is common. If you do have a relapse, don't beat yourself up. You *can* overcome your addiction. All you have to do is ask for help and get back to work on your recovery.

PREVENTING INHALANT ABUSE

According to the Alliance for Consumer Education, 87% of parents talk to their children about the dangers of alcohol, tobacco, and illegal drugs. In contrast, only 47% say that they have spoken to their children about inhalant abuse.

What You and Your Parents Can Do

The first step you should take is to educate yourself about inhalants. Find out about the different types of products that can be abused, and learn the slang names that are used to refer to them. Find out about how inhalants are used and the long- and short-term physical effects they cause.

Talk to your family doctor about the dangers of inhalants. He or she can give you up-to-date information on what inhalants can do to the body and brain.

Parents should take care to keep track of where their kids go after school and on weekends. A 2002 study by the Parents Resource Institute for Drug Education found that the majority of inhalant abuse happens at parties over the weekend. You should make sure your parents have met your friends, and let them know whom they can talk to at your school—teachers, guidance counselors, and sports coaches—if they have worries about drug use.

You and your parents should have a thorough discussion about the safe uses of the various household products that can be abused as inhalants. Any items that might be abused should be stored away from the reach of babies and small children, and use of these items should be closely monitored.

HOW TO TALK TO YOUNG PEOPLE ABOUT INHALANTS

WHAT TO SAY TO KIDS BETWEEN AGE 6 AND 11

- Explain what oxygen is and why we need it to live.
- Talk about what poisons are and how they can harm the body.
- Play games that teach kids what is safe to smell or touch.
- Explain the purpose of different household products and tell kids about how their fumes can make people sick.
- Always open windows or use products with dangerous fumes outdoors to set a good example.
- Read product labels with the child and answer any questions the child may have.
- Let the child know about the dangers of inhalants, but be careful not to explain how inhalants are used. You want to avoid giving small children ideas about how to experiment with inhalants. Inhalant abuse is learned from other people, sometimes inadvertently.

What the Community Can Do

Most communities devote a lot of time and resources to educating young people about the dangers of drugs, but they often forget to include inhalants. Communities should understand that people who abuse inhalants come from all walks of life and live in all

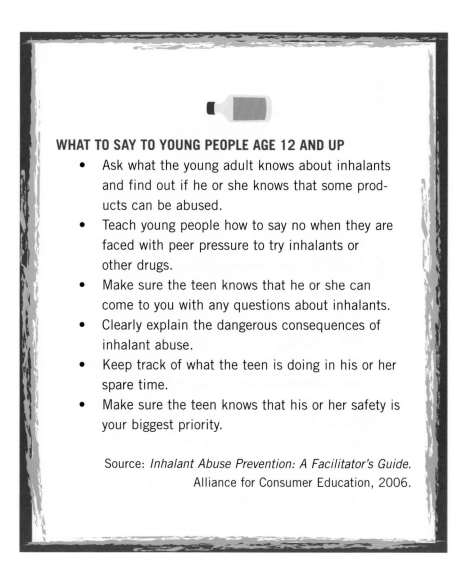

WHAT TO SAY TO YOUNG PEOPLE AGE 12 AND UP

- Ask what the young adult knows about inhalants and find out if he or she knows that some products can be abused.
- Teach young people how to say no when they are faced with peer pressure to try inhalants or other drugs.
- Make sure the teen knows that he or she can come to you with any questions about inhalants.
- Clearly explain the dangerous consequences of inhalant abuse.
- Keep track of what the teen is doing in his or her spare time.
- Make sure the teen knows that his or her safety is your biggest priority.

Source: *Inhalant Abuse Prevention: A Facilitator's Guide.* Alliance for Consumer Education, 2006.

NATIONAL INHALANTS AND POISONS AWARENESS WEEK

In March 2007, the National Inhalant Prevention Coalition (NIPC) held the first annual National Inhalants and Poisons Awareness Week. According to Harvey Weiss, the founder of NIPC, "three times the number of kids use inhalants as **meth**," yet few policymakers or parents recognize the prevalence of inhalant abuse. Weiss says that inhalants "should rank #1, because there are lots of indicators that inhalants are the first substance young people experiment with."

National Inhalants and Poisons Awareness Week, which is held during the third week of March, is a media-based program intended to inform local communities about the risks of inhalant use. The program involves schools, local police, health-care organizations, civic groups, and young people. Almost 2,000 organizations and people from 46 states took part in the 2007 event.

NIPC believes that this annual drive to educate people about inhalants will be effective because of the success of a similar state-based program used in Texas. When this program was used between 1992 and 1994, inhalant abuse among elementary schoolchildren decreased by more than 30%. Abuse among high school students decreased by more than 20%. Now that this event will take place nationally each year, NIPC and other civic groups hope that similar reductions in inhalant use will soon be seen nationwide.

types of cities and towns. Local law enforcement officials, medical professionals, and schools need to be aware of the growing problem of inhalant abuse and take steps to try to prevent young people from trying these drugs.

Discussing inhalant abuse at PTA and town meetings is a good way to make people aware of the dangers of inhalants. Inhalant abuse should be taught in schools as part of the health curriculum. Communities can spread awareness of inhalant abuse by organizing events during National Inhalants and Poison Awareness Week, which takes place every March.

Schools should make an effort to remove products that young people may steal and use as inhalants, such as certain art products or janitorial cleansers. Those products that are necessary should be closely monitored. If students are caught with inhalants, they should be recommended for counseling and treatment. If everyone—young people, parents, schools, and community leaders—works together, it becomes possible to educate the public about the little-known dangers of inhalants and ultimately decrease the rate of inhalant abuse in our country.

GLOSSARY

addiction   When the body needs a drug or other substance and suffers withdrawal symptoms if it does not get the substance

aerosols   Very fine solid particles or liquid particles suspended in gas and dispensed from a pressurized can

anaphylactic shock   A severe, often fatal, reaction to a substance, such as venom or drugs

anesthetic   A drug that sedates a person or makes a person fall asleep; used most often for surgical procedures

antifreeze   A substance added to a liquid to lower its freezing point

apathetic   Being uninterested in life

arrhythmia   An abnormal rhythm in the heartbeat

belligerent   Having an aggressive or fighting attitude

blackouts   Losses of memory, perhaps as well as vision and consciousness

carbon   A chemical element found in coal, petroleum, and asphalt, and in organic compounds

cardiac arrest   A heart attack; a temporary or permanent stoppage of the heartbeat

central nervous system   The brain and spinal cord

cerebellum   The part of the brain located between the brain stem and the back of the cerebrum; it is concerned with the coordination of the muscles and with balance

cerebral cortex   The surface layer of the cerebrum of the brain that handles sensory and motor information

chloroform   A clear, colorless liquid that can be used as a solvent to dull pain or to cause a person to lose consciousness

chromosomes   Rod-shaped or threadlike structures in cells that contain DNA

circulatory system   The organs and body parts that move the blood through the body, including the heart, blood, and blood vessels

cirrhosis   A condition that scars the liver, often caused by alcohol or other drug abuse

cognitive   Relating to thoughts and intellectual activity

coma   A state of prolonged unconsciousness caused by injury, disease, or poison

compounds   Substances formed by the union of two or more elements. For example, water is a compound formed of hydrogen and oxygen.

convulsions   A violent, involuntary contraction of the muscles

CPR   Cardiopulmonary resuscitation; a procedure designed to help start the heart and breathing after a person has suffered cardiac arrest

dementia   A condition marked by deteriorating cognitive functioning

depressants   Drugs that slow down the functions of the body

detoxification   Freeing the body of drugs

digestive system   The organs and glands that process food, including the stomach and the intestines

electrolyte   A chemical that helps regulate metabolism

ether   A flammable liquid that was used often in the nineteenth century as an anesthetic

euphoria   A feeling of extreme happiness or excitement

fault   A fracture in the crust of the Earth

fetal alcohol syndrome   Birth defects, including physical malformations and mental retardation, caused by excessive alcohol consumption by a woman during pregnancy

glaucoma   A disease of the eye marked by increased pressure inside the eyeball; it may lead to blindness

hallucinations   A belief in seeing nonrealistic objects, usually arising from use of drugs or a disorder of the nervous system

hangovers   Unpleasant physical effects caused by consuming too much alcohol or drugs

hepatitis   A disease in which the liver becomes inflamed

HIV/AIDS   Human immunodeficiency virus (HIV); acquired immunodeficiency syndrome (AIDS); HIV is a virus that causes the immune system to become weakened, eventually leading to AIDS. AIDS is a condition in which a person's body is unable to fight off illnesses because of a severely weakened immune system.

huffing   A slang term for using inhalants

hypnotic   Able to cause someone to fall asleep

immune system   The body's system for fighting off disease

infectious diseases   Diseases that can be passed from one person to another

inflammation   A reaction to injury in which the injured body part becomes red, warm, swollen, and painful

intoxicated   Drunk or high

kidney stones   Calcium-based deposits in the kidneys

lethargic   Slow; low in energy

leukemia   A cancer of the blood

lubricants   Substances that reduce friction between solid surfaces, such as components of a car engine

meth   Short for methamphetamine, a highly addictive stimulant drug

myelin sheath   A layer of fatty material that surrounds and protects certain nerve fibers

nervous system   The brain, spinal cord, and all the nerves of the body

neurological   Relating to the nervous system and its structures and functions

neurons   Nerve cells found in the brain

nitrites   Stimulant drugs sometimes used to treat chest pain but more often abused as inhalants

nitrous oxide   A colorless gas that dulls pain when inhaled

organic   Relating to living organisms

palpitations   Rapid heartbeats

paranoid   Believing that you're being punished or watched, or that certain people are out to get you

paraphernalia   Personal items, in this case associated with drug use

peripheral nerves   The nerves found outside of the central nervous system (the brain and spinal cord)

pesticide   A chemical used to kill pests, such as insects

pharmacological   Having to do with using drugs to treat a disease or condition

pneumonia   A lung infection

poisons   Substances that kill, injure, or harm a living thing

psychoactive   Affecting the mind or the way a person behaves

psychopathic   Mentally ill or unstable

scurvy   A disease caused by a lack of vitamin C that can make the gums spongy and loosen teeth

sedative   A drug that relaxes the body

seizures   Sudden attacks caused by abnormal electrical discharges in the brain that usually make the body convulse or a person lose consciousness

shamans   Religious leaders and healers in many Native American and other cultures

solvent   A liquid that can dissolve other substances

stimulants   Substances that speed up the functioning of the body

stupor   A condition in which the senses are dulled

sudden sniffing death syndrome   The most common form of death associated with inhalants; it usually occurs when the user is surprised while inhaling, causing a release of the hormone epinephrine, which can speed up the heart rate and cause cardiac arrest

tolerance   The body's ability to become less responsive to the effects of a drug that is taken over a period of time, requiring the user to take larger amounts of the same drug to achieve the same effect

toxic   Poisonous

truancy   Staying out of school without permission

vasodilators   Substances that widen the blood vessels

volatile solvents   Solvents that evaporate easily at relatively low temperatures

wasting   Decaying or losing strength

withdrawal   The often painful physical and psychological symptoms that occur when a person stops taking a drug on which his or her body has become dependent

BIBLIOGRAPHY

ARTICLES AND GUIDES

Alliance for Consumer Education. *Inhalant Abuse Prevention: A Facilitator's Guide*. Washington, D.C. 2006.

Alliance for Consumer Education. *What Every Parent Needs to Know About Inhalant Abuse*. Washington, D.C. 2006.

Ball, P. "Oracle's Secret Fault Found." Nature.com. Available online at www.nature.com/nsu/010719/010719–10.html.

Burk, I. Inhalant Prevention Resource Guide. Virginia Department of Education. Richmond, Va. 2001.

Bauerlein, M. "The Sweet Smell of Success." CityPages. http://pangaea.org/street_children/latin/citypg1.htm.

Chepesiuk, R. "Resurgence of Teen Inhalant Use." *Environmental Health Perspectives* 113 (2005): A808–A811.

Curley, B. "As Inhalant Group Marks Anniversary, Founder Airs Hopes, Concerns." *Join Together*. http://www.jointogether .org/news/features/2007/as-inhalant-group-marks.html.

Haverkos, H.W., Kopstein, A.N., et al. "Nitrite Inhalants: History, Epidemiology, and Possible Links to AIDS." *Environmental Health Perspectives* 102 (1994): 858–861.

MacDonald, J. "Groups Work to Ban Inhaled Alcohol Device in Kentucky." WAVE-3 TV, Louisville, Ky. http://www. wave3.com/Global/story.asp?s=5715291

Macksey-Amiti, M.E., Fendrich, M. "Inhalant Use and Delinquent Behavior Among Adolescents: A Comparison of Inhalant Users and Other Drug Users." *Addiction*. 94(4)(1999): 555–564.

McGarvey, E.L., Clavet G.J., et al. "Adolescent Inhalant Abuse: Environments of Use." *The American Journal of Drug and Alcohol Abuse* 25(1999): 731–741.

Mosher, C., Rotolo, T., et al. "Minority Adolescents and Substance Abuse Use Risk/Protective Factors: A Focus on Inhalant Use." *Adolescence* 39(2004): 489–502.

Reed, B. J., and May, P.A. "Inhalant Abuse and Juvenile Delinquency: A Control Study in Albuquerque, New Mexico." *International Journal of Addiction* 19(1984): 789–803.

U.S. Department of Health and Human Services. "Inhalants." *Substance Abuse Treatment Advisory: Breaking News for the Treatment Field.* Vol. 3, Issue 1, March 2003.

Wetzstein, C. "Poignant Lessons Teach Teens About Abuse of Inhalants." *The Washington Times.* December 28, 1999.

INTERNET RESOURCES

"A Whiff of Danger: Teens Use Inhalants to Get High." The Partnership for a Drug-Free America. Available online. http://www.drugfree.org/Parent/SpotDrugUse/ A_Whiff_of_Danger.

"Awareness Week: March 18–24, 2007." National Inhalant Prevention Coalition. Available online. October 2006. http://www.inhalants.org/nipaw.htm.

"Basic Facts About Drugs: Inhalants." American Council for Drug Education. Available online. http://www.acde.org/ common/Inhalant.htm.

"Chloroform." Available online. http://www.general-anaesthesia.com/chloroform.html

"Chroming." Available online. http://www.reachout.com.au/ default.asp?ti=1311.

"Commonly Abused Products & Chemical Effects." National Inhalant Prevention Coalition. Available online. http:// www.inhalants.org/scatter.htm.

"Damage Inhalants Can Do to the Body & Brain." National Inhalant Prevention Coalition. Available online. http:// www.inhalants.org/damage.htm.

"Danger Right Under Your Nose." The Partnership for a Drug-Free America. Available online. http://www. drugfree.org/Parent/Resources/Danger_Right_Under_ Your_Nose.

"Dealing With Addiction." TeensHealth. Available online. http://www.kidshealth.org/teen/drug_alcohol/getting_help/addictions.html.

Dewey, S.L. "Huffing: What Parents Should Know About Inhalant Abuse." *Reclaiming Children and Youth.* 11 (2002). Available online at http://www.accessmylibrary.com.

"Genuine Concern, Green Manufacturing." Falcon Safety Products. Available online. http://www.falconsafety.com/default.aspx?pageid=5.

"History of Inhalants." History House. Available online. http://www.inhalant-abuse.net/inhalants-history.htm.

"History of Inhalants." Spencer Recovery Centers, Inc. Available online. http://www.inhalants.net/history-of-inhalants.htm.

"History of Nitrous Oxide." Available online. http://www.manbit.com/obstetspain/n2o2.htm.

"Huffing: A Chemistry Class for Parents." HealthAtoZ. Available online. http://www.healthatoz.com.

"Huffing—An Interview With Harvey Weiss." DrugStory.org. Available online. http://www.drugstory.org/feature/harvey_weiss.asp.

"'Huffing'—Inhalants." Narcotic Educational Foundation of America. Available online. www.cnoa.org/N-07.pdf.

"Inhalant Abuse." National Institute on Drug Abuse Research Report Series. Available online. http://www.nida.nih.gov/ResearchReports/Inhalants/Inhalants4.html.

Inhalant Abuse Fact Sheet. Partnership for a Drug-Free America. 2006. Available online. http://www.drugfree.org/Parent/Resources/Inhalant_Abuse_Fact_Sheet.

"Inhalant Abuse: Help Your Child Understand the Risks." MayoClinic.com. Available online. http://www.mayoclinic.com/health/inhalant-abuse/HQ00923.

"Inhalant Exposure." The Children's Hospital of Philadelphia. Available online. http://www.chop.edu/consumer/jsp/division/generic.jsp?id=70989.

"Inhalant Use Increases Among Girls." *Casper Star Tribune*. March 16, 2007. Available online. http://www.casperstartribune.net.

"Inhalants." Center for Substance Abuse Research. Available online. http://www.cesar.unmd.edu/cesar/drugs/inhalants.asp.

"Inhalants." Children's Hospital of Pittsburgh. Available online. http://www.kidshealth.org.

"Inhalants." Cyswllt Ceredigion Contact. Available online. http://www.recovery.org.uk/druginfo/inhale.html.

"Inhalants." Greater Dallas Council on Alcohol & Drug Abuse. Available online. http://www.gdcada.org/statistics/inhalants.htm.

"Inhalants." www.streetdrugs.org. Available online at http://www.streetdrugs.org/inhalants.htm.

"Inhalants: Drug Facts." Freevibe.com. Available online. http://www.freevibe.com/Drug_Facts/inhalants.asp.

"Inhalants Overview." Office of National Drug Control Policy. Available online. http://www.whitehousedrugpolicy.gov/drugfact/inhalants/index.html.

"Inhalants: Quick Facts." Parents: The Anti-Drug. Available online. http://www.theantidrug.com/drug_info/drug_info_inhalants_quickfacts.asp.

"Inhalants: Which Kids Do It?" MedicineNet.com. Available online. http://www.medicinenet.com.

"Jeny's Story." The Partnership for a Drug-Free America. Available online. http://www.drugfree.org/Parent/Resources/Jenys_Story.

Miller, C. "Breathable Booze: Better than Drinking?" *Daily Free Press*. September 7, 2004. Available online at http://media.www.dailyfreepress.com/media/storage/paper87/

news/2004/09/07/ScienceTuesday/Breathable.Booze.Better. Than.Drinking-711767.shtml.

"My Daughter's Huffing Addiction." The Partnership for a Drug-Free America. Available online. http://www.drugfree. org/Portal/Stories/My_Daughters_Huffing_Addiction.

"New Findings on Inhalants: Parent and Youth Attitudes—A Special Report." The Partnership for a Drug-Free America. Available online. http://www.drugfree.org/Portal/DrugIssue/ News/New_Findings_on_Inhalants_Parent_and_Youth.

"NIDA InfoFacts: Inhalants." National Institute on Drug Abuse. Available online. http://www.drugabuse.gov/ Infofacts/Inhalants.html.

"Red Ribbon Works!" Red Ribbon Resources. Available online. http://www.redribbonworks.org/resource_home. asp?parent=1&PageId=18.

"SAMHSA Issues Treatment Guidelines on Inhalants." U.S. Medicine: The Voice of Federal Medicine. Available online. http://www.usmedicine.com/dailyNews.cfm?dailyID=142.

Schaffer, A. "Vaporize Me: Is Inhalable Alcohol a Good Idea?" *Slate*. September 8, 2004. Available online at http:// www.slate.com/id/2106393/.

"Signs of Inhalant Abuse." Parents: The Anti-Drug. Available online. http://www.theantidrug.com/drug_info/drug_info_ inhalants_signs.asp.

"Solvent Abuse." The Site.org. Available online. http://www. thesite.org/drinkanddrugs/drugsafety/usingdrugs/ solventabuse.

"Solvents and Aerosols (Inhalants)." Leeds, Grenville & Lanark Health District, Ontario, Canada. Available online. http://www.healthunit.org/alcoholdrug/drugs/solvaerosols. htm.

"Solvents/Inhalants: Beyond the ABCs." Alberta Alcohol and Drug Abuse Commission. Available online. http://www. aadac.com/87_413.asp.

"Street Terms: Drugs and the Drug Trade." Office of National Drug Control Policy. Available online. http://www.whitehousedrugpolicy.gov/streetterms/.

"The Unusual History of Ether." Thomas J. Evans, CRNA, BSN, MS. Available online. http://www.anesthesia-nursing.com/ether.html.

"What a Gas: Part II." History House. Available online. http://www.historyhouse.com/in_history/nitrous_two.

"What to Do When Someone Is Huffing." National Inhalant Prevention Coalition. Available online. http://www.inhalants.org/whattodo.htm.

"Why Inhalants Are Being Used." National Inhalant Prevention Coalition. Available online. http://www.inhalants.org/whyuse.htm.

FURTHER READING

Aretha, David. *Inhalants*. Berkeley Heights, N.J.: MyReport-Links, 2005.

Bankston, John. *Inhalants = Busted!* Berkeley Heights, N.J.: Enslow Publishers, 2006.

Lawton, Sandra Augustyn, ed. *Drug Information for Teens: Health Tips About the Physical and Mental Effects of Substance Abuse*. Detroit: Omnigraphics, 2006.

Lobo, Ingrid A. *Inhalants*. Philadelphia: Chelsea House Publishers, 2004.

Marcovitz, Hal. *Inhalants*. San Diego: Lucent Books, 2005.

Menhard, Francha Roffe. *The Facts About Inhalants*. New York: Benchmark Books, 2004.

Monroe, Judy. *Inhalant Drug Dangers*. Berkeley Heights, N.J.: Enslow Publishers, 2000.

O'Donnell, Kerri. *Inhalants and Your Nasal Passages: The Incredibly Disgusting Story*. New York: Rosen, 2001.

WEB SITES

AMERICAN COUNCIL FOR DRUG EDUCATION
http://www.acde.org/common/Inhalant.htm

Learn basic facts about inhalants, including signs that someone is abusing inhalants.

INHALANT AND SOLVENT ABUSE INFORMATION
http://www.egetgoing.com/drug_rehab/inhalants_solvents.asp

How and why people use inhalants and solvents is explained.

NATIONAL INSTITUTE ON DRUG ABUSE
http://www.nida.nih.gov/Infofacts/Inhalants.html

Discover more about inhalants and how sniffing them can harm your body.

PHOTO CREDITS

INDEX

A

accidental highs, 20
acetone, 17
addiction
  gasoline and, 31
  Megan's story, 67–68
  physical, 68
  problems caused by, 71–72
  psychological, 69
  risk of, 56
  Schedule I–V substances and, 21–23
  signs of, 71
adrenaline, 53
aerosol cans, 12, 38
aerosols, 17
AIDS (acquired immunodeficiency syndrome), 48. *See also* HIV infection
air, canned, 59
air fresheners, aerosol, 33, 38
Albuquerque, New Mexico, 70
alcohol, inhalable, 42–43
alcohol abuse, 70
Alcohol Without Liquid (AWOL), 43
allergies, 54
Alliance for Consumer Education, 34, 89
amyl nitrite, 18, 20, 38, 48
anaphylactic shock, 54
anesthetic effects, 15
anesthetics, inhaled, 26–31
antifreeze, 40
anxiety, 62
arrhythmia, 53
art supplies, 35
asphyxiation, 54
auto supplies, 35
avoidance of inhalants, 64–66

B

babies, 53
bad breath, 47
bagging, 19–20

balloons, 20, 36
Beatty, Wayne, 59
behavior problems, 46, 72
behavioral signs of inhalant abuse, 74
behavioral treatment, 82–87
belligerent behavior, 46
benzene, 40, 72
blood vessels, 38
bloodstream, 46
brain damage, 49–51, 82
burn injuries, 40
butane, 17, 36, 40, 47
butyl nitrite, 18, 20, 38

C

canned air, 59
canned whipped cream, 36
carbon compounds, 17
carbon monoxide, 41
cardiac arrest, 51
cardiopulmonary resuscitation (CPR), 77
Central America, 64
central nervous system, 18, 34, 38
cerebellum, 49
cerebral cortex, 49
chemical makeup of inhalants, 40–41
chlorinated hydrocarbons, 17
chloroform, 28, 30, 36
choking, 54, 55
circulatory system, 47
cirrhosis of the liver, 41
Citizen Ruth, 64
cleaning supplies, 35
Cobain, Kurt, 64
cognitive-behavioral therapy, 85
Coleridge, Samuel Taylor, 29
coma, 54
combustion of fumes, 55
community involvement, 91–93

compounds, 17
Consumer Product Safety Commission, 38
control, in behavioral therapy, 85–86
Controlled Substances Act (1970), 20, 21–23
convulsions, 55
cooking supplies, 35
correction fluids, 20
cost of inhalants, 60–61
counseling, 78
CPR, 77
crime and inhalants, 70, 72
cyclohexyl nitrite, 38

D
Davy, Humphry, 28, 29
death
    causes of, 54
    injury, fatal, 55
    from nitrous oxide, 41
    sudden sniffing death syndrome, 13, 40, 41, 53–54
    suicide, 56
Delphi, oracle of Apollo at, 24–26
dentistry, 28–30
Depp, Johnny, 64
depressants, inhalants as, 45–46
depression, 56, 62
detoxification, 81–82
digestive system, 15, 46
disorientation, 60
dizziness, 60
dung sniffing, 63–64
dusting, 59

E
Ecstasy, 14, 32
effects of inhalants
    chemical makeup and, 40–41
    long-term, 49–53
    other risks, 54–57
    short-term, 45–49

sudden sniffing death syndrome as, 53–54
emergency room visits, 56–57
emotional problems, 62
epinephrine, 53
ether, 26–28, 36
ethylene, 26
euphoria, 26, 46

F
fads, 44
family, 86–87
fatal injury, 55. *See also* death
faults, 26
Fear and Loathing in Las Vegas (Thompson), 64
fingernails, 20
flammability, 40, 55
fluorocarbons, 17
freon, 40, 47
friends, 86. *See also* peer pressure
Fries, Katelyne, 12–13
fright, danger from, 76–77

G
gases, 18, 35–36
gasoline, 31, 40, 64, 71
gateway drugs, inhalants as, 44
gay men, 47–49
general supplies, 35
girls, increase in inhalant abuse in, 59
glaucoma, 53
glue, 31, 64
glue-sniffer's rash, 51
groups, huffing in, 61

H
hallucinations, 26, 53
hallucinogenic drugs, 14
halothane, 36
hangovers, 43, 47
headaches, 53
health and beauty supplies, 35

hearing loss, 51
heart, 51
helium, 36
help and treatment
  behavioral treatment,
    82–87
  detoxification, 81–82
  difficulty finding treatment,
    80–81
  drug addiction treatment,
    77–80
  organizations offering help,
    75
  pharmacological treatment,
    82
  SAMHSA guidelines, 83–84
  tips for recovery, 87–89
  warning signs, 73–76
  what to do if someone you
    know is abusing, 76–77
highs, 43–44, 58–60
history of inhalant use
  in ancient times, 24–26
  anesthetics, 26–31
  recreational drug use, 31–32
  today, 32
HIV infection, 41, 48, 49. *See
also* AIDS (acquired immunodeficiency syndrome)
homosexual men, 47–49
household products, 15, 31–32,
  36–37, 60
huffing
  in groups, 61
  Katelyne Fries and Kyle Wil-
    liams, 12–13
  method of, 19
  sudden sniffing death syn-
    drome and, 53
hydrocarbons, chlorinated, 17
hypnotic effects, 15

I

immune system, 40
incense, 26

infectious diseases, 71, 80
inhalant, defined, 34
injury, fatal, 55
intoxication, 25

J

Joplin, Janis, 64
Journal of Substance Abuse, 70

K

kidney stones, 51
kidneys, 51, 71

L

"Lacquer Head" (Primus), 64
"laughing gas" (nitrous oxide),
  18, 28–31, 36, 41, 52
leather cleaner, 38
leukemia, 40, 51
liver, 51, 72
Long, Crawford, 26
lubricants, 41
Lullius, Raymundus, 26
lungs, 72

M

marijuana, 32
mental illness, 78
methadone, 81
methylene chloride, 41, 51
Minnitt, Ralph, 30
model airplane glue, 31
movies, 64
multidimensional family therapy (MDFT), 86
muscle wasting, 51
myelin sheath, 49

N

National Inhalant Prevention
  Coalition (NIPC), 92
National Inhalants and Poisons
  Awareness Week, 92, 93

National Institute on Drug
   Abuse (NIDA), 58–59, 62, 78,
   85
National Survey on Drug Use
   and Health (SAMHSA), 14
Native Americans, 26
Natrona County School District,
   Wyoming, 59
nerves, peripheral, 52
nervous system, 15, 18, 34, 38
neurons, 49
nitrites
   about, 18, 38
   infectious diseases and, 71
   long-term effects of, 51
   short-term effects of, 47–49
   as type of inhalant, 17
nitrous oxide ("laughing gas"),
   18, 28–31, 36, 41, 52
"Now I Wanna Sniff Some Glue"
   (The Ramones), 64

O
ophthalmic nerve, 51
oracle of Apollo at Delphi,
   24–26
organic solvents, 17, 19, 51
organizations offering help, 75
OxyContin, 32

P
paranoia, 46
paraphernalia, 61
parents, 89–90
Parents Resource Institute for
   Drug Education, 89
parties, 29, 88–89
patterns of inhalant use, 62–66
peer groups, new, 87
peer pressure, 59, 61
peripheral nerves, 52
pesticide, 41
pharmacological treatment, 82
physical signs of inhalant abuse,
   74

poisons, 15, 51
poppers, 18, 38, 48
popular culture, inhalants in,
   63, 64
popularity of inhalants, 41–44,
   60–61
pregnancy, 53, 72
preventing inhalant abuse
   talking about it, 89, 90–91
   what the community can do,
      91–93
   what you and your parents
      can do, 89–90
Priestley, Joseph, 28
Primus, 64
principles of treatment,
   78–80
profile of an inhalant user, 14
programs for treatment. See help
   and treatment
propane, 17, 36, 40, 47
propellants, 38. See also aerosol
   cans
psychoactive effects, 26
psychological addiction, 69
psychological problems, 56, 62
psychotherapy, 82

R
The Ramones, 64
rashes, 51
recreational drugs, inhalants as,
   31–32
red blood cells, 41
rehab, 68, 81. See also help and
   treatment
relapse, 82, 85, 89
reproductive system, 40
Roget, Peter, 29

S
Schedule I substances, 21
Schedule II substances, 21
Schedule III substances, 22
Schedule IV substances, 22

Schedule V substances, 22–23
school, problems in, 70
school involvement, 93
scurvy, 26
sedative effects, 15
seizures, 55
sex-related dangers, 55
sexual behavior, 41, 47–49,
    55–56
sexually transmitted diseases
    (STDs), 56
shamans, 26
signs of inhalant abuse, 69,
    73–76
situational signs of inhalant
    abuse, 76
social control, 86
solvents
    defined, 34
    as inhalants, 15
    organic, 17, 19, 51
    volatile, 17
South America, 64
Southeast Asia, 63–64
speech effects, 46
startling, danger from, 53,
    76–77
stimulants, nitrites as, 47
stimulus control, 85–86
street names for inhalants, 39
Substance Abuse and Mental
    Health Service Administration
    (SAMHSA), 14, 59, 83–84
sudden sniffing death syn-
    drome (SSDS), 13, 40, 41,
    53–54
suffocation, 55
suicide, 56
swallowing bags, risk of, 55

T
talking to young people about
    inhalants, 90–91

Themis (priestess), 24
Thompson, Hunter S., 64
tolerance, 56, 68
toluene
    effects of, 40, 47, 51, 52–53,
        71
    sources of, 17, 31
toxicity, 71
treatment. See help and treat-
    ment
tricloroethylene, 40–41
triggers, 85
truancy, 70

U
unconsciousness, 77
urge control, 86

V
vasodilators, 18
Venable, James, 26
video head cleaner, 38
violent behavior, 46, 72
vision problems, 51, 53
volatile solvents, 17

W
warning signs of inhalant
    abuse, 73–76
Weiss, Harvey, 92
Wells, Horace, 28–30
whipped cream, canned,
    36
withdrawal, 53
withdrawal symptoms, 68, 71,
    79, 81
wood shop supplies, 35

Y
Youth Risk Behavior Surveil-
    lance Survey, 14

ABOUT THE AUTHORS

TARA KOELLHOFFER earned a degree in political science and history from Rutgers University. Today, she is a freelance writer and editor with more than 10 years of experience working on nonfiction books, covering topics ranging from social studies and biography to health and science. She has edited hundreds of books and teaching materials, including a history of Italy published by Greenhaven Press and the *Science News for Kids* series published by Chelsea House. She lives in Pennsylvania with her husband, Gary.

Series introduction author **RONALD J. BROGAN** is the Bureau Chief for the New York City office of D.A.R.E. (Drug Abuse Resistance Education) America, where he trains and coordinates more than 100 New York City police officers in program-related activities. He also serves as a D.A.R.E. regional director for Oregon, Connecticut, Massachusetts, Maine, New Hampshire, New York, Rhode Island, and Vermont. In 1997, Brogan retired from the U.S. Drug Enforcement Administration (DEA), where he served as a special agent for 26 years. He holds bachelor's and master's degrees in criminal justice from the City University of New York.